Death and Funeral Practices in Russia

Built on original ethnographic research conducted by the author, this book offers a highly detailed and comprehensive account of funerary history and practices in Russia. *Death and Funeral Practices in Russia* provides rich data on mortality statistics, trends in the funeral market in contemporary Russia, the legal framework of funerary practices, as well as regional and demographic disparities.

The first part of the book presents an in-depth account of the historical development of funerary practice in Russia, charting the emergence and evolution of funeral traditions and customs in the country from the Russian Empire to the collapse of the USSR. Having explored the wider historical context surrounding funerary culture in Russia, the second part of the book explores the key features of the funeral industry in post-Soviet times, highlighting critical changes and areas of continuity. Topics explored include the death care industry in Russia, the key features of the typical funeral in the country, cemetery and crematorium provision, the technicalities and legalities of burial and cremation, and the illegal practices within the funeral market.

A truly unique offering, the book is essential reading for academics, policy makers and practitioners interested in the history and legal, technical and professional aspects of the funerary industry in Russia.

Sergei Mokhov is Research Fellow in the Institute of Ethnology and Anthropology at the Russian Academy of Science, Russia, and at Liverpool John Moores University, UK.

Routledge International Focus on Death and Funeral Practices

Series Editor – Julie Rugg
University of York, UK

Death Studies is an international and interdisciplinary endeavour and encompasses an interest in all mortality-related themes. This series of shortform books provides essential information on death and funeral practices in countries throughout the world.

Creating a common framework for understanding funeral rituals rests on definition and the description of processes, events and rituals which ostensibly appear the same but in actuality are markedly different, country to country. Each book has the same basic structure, which incorporates:

- historic, contextual background to understand how funeral practices have developed;
- burial and cremation rates, and change over time;
- an outline of key legislation guiding death registration, the funeral industry and cemetery and crematorium provision;
- what happens in the event of a death;
- an overview of the funeral industry including the ways in which funeral directing services are delivered and the balance of state/private involvement in funeral directing business;
- the cost of funerals and how they are paid for;
- church involvement in funerals and arrangements made for minority religious groups;
- a full and detailed description of a typical funeral;
- the provision of cemetery and crematorium services;
- patterns of commemoration

Fully referenced, and supported by relevant images, figures and tables, books in the series provide an essential research resource on practices, the law, and funeral-related procedures around the world. Collectively, the series provides an invaluable framework for international comparison.

This series is a continuation of *Funerary International*, a series distributed by Emerald Publishing. Four books were published in this legacy series: *Funerary Practices in England and Wales* (Rugg & Parsons, 2018); *Funerary Practices in the Netherlands* (Mathijssen & Venhorst, 2019), *Funerary Practices in the Czech Republic* (Nešporová 2021; and *Funerary Practices in Serbia* (Pavićević,2021).

Death and Funeral Practices in Russia
Sergei Mokhov

For more information on the series please visit: www.routledge.com/Routledge-International-Focus-on-Death-and-Funeral-Practices/book-series/DEATH

Death and Funeral Practices in Russia

Sergei Mokhov

Routledge
Taylor & Francis Group

LONDON AND NEW YORK

First published 2022
by Routledge
2 Park Square, Milton Park, Abingdon, Oxon OX14 4RN

and by Routledge
605 Third Avenue, New York, NY 10158

Routledge is an imprint of the Taylor & Francis Group, an informa business

British Library Cataloguing-in-Publication Data
A catalogue record for this book is available from the British Library

Library of Congress Cataloging-in-Publication Data
Names: Mokhov, Sergei, author.
Title: Death and funeral practices in Russia / Sergei Mokhov.
Description: New York : Routledge, 2022. | Series: Routledge
    International Focus on Death and Funeral Practices | Includes
    bibliographical references and index.
Identifiers: LCCN 2021041227 (print) | LCCN 2021041228 (ebook)
Subjects: LCSH: Funeral rites and ceremonies—Russia—History. |
    Death care industry—Russia. | Mourning etiquette—Russia.
Classification: LCC GT3256.A2 M65 2022 (print) | LCC GT3256.
    A2 (ebook) | DDC 393/.930947—dc23/eng/20211014
LC record available at https://lccn.loc.gov/2021041227
LC ebook record available at https://lccn.loc.gov/2021041228

ISBN: 978-0-367-72152-7 (hbk)
ISBN: 978-0-367-72153-4 (pbk)
ISBN: 978-1-003-15367-2 (ebk)

DOI: 10.4324/9781003153672

Typeset in Times
by Apex CoVantage, LLC

Contents

Illustrations

Figures

Table

Map

Boxes

Preface

It is a very uncommon situation when a separate country constitutes the whole object for social discipline. The more familiar way is to study a region or particular historical period: for example, Pacific studies or Central Asian studies, modern European history. However, when it comes to Russia, it ceases to be true. Russia has always been a particular object of research and forms a research field – 'Russian studies'. Dozens of centers in the world's leading universities are studying specifically Russian literature, history, and social structure. Why is it so?

At first glance, the reason for such exoticization lies in a specific pathway of Western anthropology. In particular, it is the heritage of the colonial world system and the place of anthropological knowledge in the 'bipolar' world order in the first half of the 20th century. At that time, scholars tended to group countries into three big classes: the First World (consisting of the USA, Western Europe, and their allies); the Second World, the so-called Communist Bloc (including the Soviet Union, China, and Cuba); and the Third World, the remaining countries, which aligned with neither of the groups. In this point of view, Russia (USSR) took a unique 'middle' position between two different systems: Western ex-Empires and their ex-colonies.

Now this framework looks simplified. We must agree that scholars use more extended models that were updated under the influence of decolonial critique. As a result, uniqueness was attributed to all countries, however, with an appeal to their past – colonial or imperial. In this focus, we may assume that Western knowledge about Russia has to be decolonized as well. However, this has never happened. We continue to talk about Russia as something exceptional. In this regard, this book's topic – funeral practices in Russia – will also be rather unusual and will contain quite shocking descriptions. These descriptions will indicate a big difference between the Western view on the funeral system and Russia's 'specific' way.

I have mentioned the discussion about the 'special Russian way' for practical reasons. There are no official statistics about the funeral industry in contemporary Russia. It means that there is a lack of data in many quantitative parameters. One prominent Russian sociologist and government advisor, Simon Kordosky, noted that 'Russian state administrators do not know how Russia is living'. We have to recognize that the Russian statistical system works very poorly and requires massive digitalization of data.

As a result of this lack, the major part of data which I am going to present will be based on a long-running ethnographic observation between 2015 and 2017 in several regions of the Russian Federation (Kaluga Region, Tula Region, Orel Region, Kursk Region, Lipetsk Region, Stary Oskol, Moscow, and Moscow Region). This study involved describing and interpreting the professional activities of five funeral agencies in these regions. Other actors took part in interactions and funeral activities as well, including dozens of cemeteries, mortuaries, manufacturers of funeral accessories, and so forth.

This book also encompasses data from archival sources – the Russian State Historical Archive (RGIA), the Russian State Archive of Moscow Region (RGAMO), as well as archival data from other researchers and data from open sources. It assisted in reconstructing the process of institutionalization of the funeral business in Russia at different stages.

The empirical data are supplemented by a qualitative analysis of the Russian laws and regulations related to the issues of development and operation of the funeral business in Russia. The data are also enriched by other regulatory documents, including available statistics on the issue under consideration. Using such a broad range of tools and an extensive empirical base allowed us to generalize the findings, going beyond the regional framework and the narrow ethnographic description of specific organizations.

Acknowledgments

I want to express my gratitude to the people without whom this book would not be possible. These are my family and friends who put up with my fieldwork at a funeral agency (2015–2018). Thanks to my colleagues, Anna Sokolova and Daria Milenina, for their advice and help in working on the text. Special thanks to Ilya Boltunov, the funeral director, who introduced me to the field. Julie Rugg, a special thanks to you for your offer to make this book – it is a great honour for me.

The book was recommended for publishing by the Academic Council of the IEA RAS

1 The Russia

An introduction

1.1 Russia in historical perspective: key points

The official history of Russia spans more than 1000 years and draws its pathway from Kievan Rus' (9–13th centuries), through the Grand Duchy of Moscow and Tsardom of Russia (12–17th centuries), the Russian Empire (18–20th centuries), the USSR (20th century), to the Russian Federation (20th century–present). I will briefly talk about the last 300 years of Russia's development. This particular time period has had the greatest impact on modern funeral practices in Russia.

The Russian historical pathway, in comparison with other European countries, seems extraordinary. Despite its current role as a 'catch-up' country, the Russian Empire was the biggest and most powerful empire on the European continent and exerted a significant influence on the European civilization – from culture to political aspects. The 'Big Soviet Experiment" fixed Russia's pathway as a unique case for the entire world. It was the first time in world history that a whole country attempted to build a socialist state. Despite all the negative expectations, the USSR became one of the world leaders and asserted influence on the world system from science to culture. After the collapse of the USSR in 1991, contemporary Russia proceeded in a different way from Western countries. The last 30 years of Russian domestic and foreign policy serve as a clear example of it: experts agreed on the failure of democratic transition and started talking about the 'special path' for Russia again. As The World FactBook describes:

> Following economic and political turmoil during President Boris Yeltsin's term (1991–99), Russia shifted toward a centralized authoritarian state under President Vladimir Putin (2000–2008, 2012-present) in which the regime seeks to legitimize its rule through managed elections, populist appeals, a foreign policy focused on enhancing the country's geopolitical influence, and commodity-based economic growth.[1]

DOI: 10.4324/9781003153672-1

We will not go into all the political and social transformations over this long time and will focus briefly only on characteristics that are important for understanding funeral practices in Russia. Let us underline several social and political features that may assist in grasping funeral development in Russian history:

- The history of Russia and the Orthodox Church especially has not encompassed such severe dogmatic crises and transformations as the Reformation in Europe, which led to wars, social disruption, and political transformations. Of course, the schism in the Orthodox Church in the 17th century resulted in the marginalization of the Old Believers and had severe consequences on Russian society. However, unlike the Reformation, the schism did not cause profound changes. The traditional Christian concept of the place of the dead in a spiritual realm remained unchanged until the end of the 19th century. Throughout the existence of the Russian Empire, the clergy was a privileged, almost closed estate. Despite the radical secularization carried out by the USSR, religious views remained an essential part of the traditional peasant culture.[2]
- The Russian Empire occupied vast spaces, and urbanization happened extremely slowly: cities were located at great distances, and the mobility of residents was low. By this type of economy, the Russian Empire and the Russian city at the beginning of the 20th century remained agricultural. Peasants made up 80 percent of the total population. The high level of the peasantry of Russia has always harmed its advancement. In comparison with other European empires, the Russian Empire lagged behind on a number of parameters.[3]
- Soviet urbanization did not lead to the emergence of urban culture and, according to the Russian historian Boris Mironov, 'turned Soviet cities into large villages'.[4] The urban culture (one of the most critical factors in the formation of the funeral industry in Europe) did not receive proper development in Russia.[5] If European culture is an urban culture, then the culture of the Russian Empire and the USSR still remained rural, with predominantly archaic features in large cities.
- The Russian economy has always been built on the sale of natural resources (gas, oil, forest, diamonds, furs), which negatively affected the development of high technologies. Industrialization reached the Russian Empire relatively late and until the end of the 18th century did not find state support. The middle class in the Russian Empire was represented mainly by lower middle class (artisans, teachers, artists), which became a noticeable layer of the population only on the cusp of the 19th and 20th centuries.[6] In Soviet times, the private entrepreneurial

initiative was subject not only to public censorship but also to criminal prosecution. The middle class, as the leading consumer of funeral services, has not formed.

- In Russian culture, informal (traditional) relationships are very important. The level of tolerance for corruption is high.[7] Corruption is perceived as a part of the practices of gift exchange.
- The political culture of Russia was also quite specific. An authoritarian monarchy regime was preserved until the October Revolution, and a system of democratic representation was not developed. In the USSR, the experience of active participation of citizens was quickly curtailed; political activists were subjected to repression. In modern Russia, there is also a reasonably authoritarian political regime. We can say that the institutions of democracy in Russia are still not advanced. Also, social mobility has been deficient throughout Russia's history.

Summing up, we can conclude that the primary institutional factors for the formation and improvement of the funeral industry (market economy, urbanization, middle class) simply failed to develop.

1.2 Contemporary Russia: an overview

The Russian Federation ranks first in the world in terms of territory size (17,125,191 km), which is slightly smaller than the continent of South America. On the other hand, the population of contemporary Russia is about 145 million people, which is comparable to the population of Japan. Both of these factors (population/territory) make Russia the most sparsely populated country in the world: the major part of the country is the uninhabited tundra and taiga. The population density is 8.57 people/km². This means that funerary infrastructure is highly dispersed.[8]

Russia is a federative and multiethnic state which includes more than 160 different ethnic groups. The ethnic groups of Russia speak more than 100 languages and dialects belonging to the Indo-European, Altai, and Uralic language families, Caucasian and Paleo-Asian language groups. The most common languages are Russian, Tatar, Chechen, Bashkir, Ukrainian, and Chuvash. Russian is the mother tongue of approximately 130 million Russian citizens (92 percent of the Russian population).

Christians (mainly Orthodox), Muslims, Buddhists, Jews, as well as representatives of other religious movements live in Russia. According to the PEW research center, the proportion of Russian citizens who identify themselves as Orthodox Christians is about 60 percent. Russian culture is quite religious, despite the fact that a small percentage of people attend church services.[9]

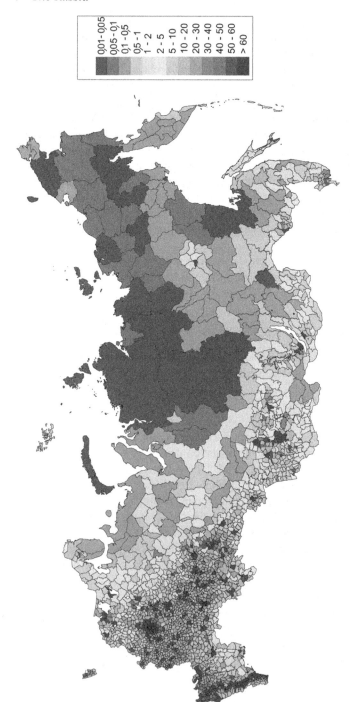

Map 1.1 Population density of Russian Federation.

Source: Kiushkina, Violetta and Lukutin, Boris. 2019. Energy security of northern and arctic isolated territories. E3S Web of Conferences.

As a result, it is hard to pinpoint some general 'Russian characteristics'. For instance, the difference between Central Russia and the Caucasus is rather significant. So, where is it possible I will mark such differences, but here generally we will speak about Central Russia.

1.3 Political system

The state system of modern Russia is built on the principles of federalism. The state is governed by the president, the prime minister at the head of the cabinet of ministers, the State Duma, and the Federation Council. The Russian Federation consists of 85 subdivisions (entities) – 22 republics, 9 krais, 46 oblasts, 3 federal cities, 1 autonomous oblast, and 4 autonomous okrugs. The entities of the federation have their own departments of executive and legislative power and of the judiciary but have limited autonomy in making law, economy, taxes. Each entity of the Federation is divided into local municipalities. There are about 21,541 municipalities in Russia. Municipalities are local governments that are engaged in economic and infrastructural activities (including the adoption of laws for this).

However, Russian federalism is unique. Regions cannot elect their leaders. Russian political researcher Yevgeny Gontmakher notes that 'Russian Federation is a spontaneously formed confederation which is characterized by 1) an extremely weak working federal legislative base and a variety of special statuses of the regions'.[10] Many researchers define the political regime of modern Russia as 'hybrid', consisting of democratic authoritarian institutions. This means that de jure it is democracy and local self-government, and de facto it is authoritarianism. For the theme of this book, the main point here is that municipalities run local services.

1.4 Social, cultural, economic context

The population of Russia constitutes 74 percent rural and 26 percent urban; 170 cities have a population of more than 100,000 people, and 15 cities have a population of more than 1 million people.[11] Thus, the Russian Federation is a country with a weakly urbanized population. The main settlement type is small cities, where residents live in low-rise housing and are often employed in the agricultural economic sector. Most of the population of Russia is concentrated in the central resettlement zone – the triangle, with three peaks being St. Petersburg in the north, Sochi in the south, and Irkutsk in the east. To the north of this favorable climatic-conditions triangle lies the zone of taiga and permafrost; to the southeast, an area of semi-deserts and deserts.

As of February 2020, the unemployment rate is 5.0 percent, and the employment rate is 59.3 percent.[12] The average nominal salary of an employee in Russia in January 2016 amounted to 32,122 ₽ per month (approximately $500). Most of Russia's economically active population works in the shadow economy (service industry, small-scale production). Market relations are weak. Most economic sectors are monopolized by the state or divided between large players. The average salary in the constituent entities of the Russian Federation corresponds to the average salary in some African countries. Most people live in relatively poor conditions. Nearly 20 million people live below the poverty line. A social group with low and meager incomes makes up about 30 percent of the total population, except for large cities such as Moscow, St. Petersburg, and Yekaterinburg. In Russia, the middle class has always been absent, or its number insignificant.

Family is quite significant in modern Russia. In general, we can say that the conventional view of the family prevails. It applies to familiar gender roles, household management strategies, and distribution of the family budget. Often several generations of one family live in the same apartment/house. The role of bonds between distant relatives and participation in the annual ritual life is stable. It has an impact on the funeral industry: many relatives take part in the funerals, and this is an essential part of community life.

Thus, speaking of a very average portrait of a consumer of funeral services, we can assume that they are:

- White Russian,
- Orthodox,
- has a low-income level,
- has a large family with which he/she maintains relations,
- lives in Central Russia, and
- lives in a small city (most cities in Russia have a population of 20,000 to 200,000) with a poorly developed urban culture.

1.5 Demography and mortality

Russia ranks tenth in the mortality rate among all countries of the world. Almost 2 million people die in Russia every year. The population decline is 200,000 people annually. Men tend to die earlier than women. In 2013, the World Health Organization released an annual report which stated that the life expectancy of Russian men is the lowest among the population of Europe and Central Asia: Russian men live on average only 67.5 years (and 77.5 for women).[13]

Most of the dying people in Russia die from chronic heart diseases (50 percent), cancer is the second position (15 percent), and the 'external causes of death' are third (10 percent). The third category includes accidents, murders, suicides, and injuries. About 20,000 people die in road accidents per year, and the same number dies from diabetes. Ten out of a thousand die from violence. This figure is ten times more than in China, the United Kingdom, and Egypt, but two times less than in Latin America. A significant problem that increases mortality is the high level of alcohol and drug usage. In Russia, about 3 million people are active drug users. Almost three-quarters of all HIV infections in Eastern Europe and Central Asia belong to the Russian Federation.[14]

Paradoxically, throughout the 20th century life expectancy has improved little, with a decrease in the number of the dying. The reasons lie in social and economic upheavals – world wars and political repression – low levels of urbanization, and the late implementation of a public health program. As it has been mentioned, according to the statistics, about 20 million Russians live below the poverty line. Several million people do not have access to clean drinking water and sanitation. The highest mortality rate is reported in Central Russia and the lowest in Siberia and Russian North.[15]

According to the study by The Economist Intelligence Unit (2018), the Russian healthcare model ranks among the least effective, at the level of Nigeria, Brazil, and South Africa.[16] Poor performance can be explained by low funding of Russian healthcare, which affects the quality of life. In terms of quality of life, Russia in this rating occupies 72nd place out of 80 (2013).[17] Despite the development of a clinical culture, the principal place of death for most Russians is their place of residence.

Notes

1 The World Factbook. Central Intelligence Agency. www.cia.gov/library/publi cations/the-world-factbook/geos/rs.html acc. May 18, 2020.
2 Thomas Bremer (2013) *Cross and Kremlin: A Brief History of the Orthodox Church in Russia*. Grand Rapids, MI: Eerdmans; Gregory L. Freeze (2008) 'Recent scholarship on Russian Orthodoxy: A critique', *Kritika: Explorations in Russian and Eurasian History*, 2:2, 269–278.
3 According to the professor at the University of California G. Grossman, the volume of industrial production in Russia in 1913 per capita constituted 1/10 of the corresponding indicator of the USA. G. Grossman (1960) *Soviet Statistics of Physical Output of Industrial Commodities: Their Compilation and Quality*. Princeton, NJ: Princeton University Press. The size of Russia's gross domestic product per capita in 1913, according to the American economic historian P. Gregory, was 50 percent of the corresponding German and French, 1/5 – of the English. Gregory, P. (1976) '1913 Russian national income: Some insights into Russian economic development', *The Quarterly Journal of Economics*, 90:3, 445–459.
4 Boris Mironov (2012) 'Gorod iz derevni: chetyresta let rossijskoj urbanizacii', *Otechestvennye zapiski*, 3:48, 111.
5 C. Becker, J. Mendelsohn and K. Benderskaya (2012) *Russian Urbanization in the Soviet and Post-Soviet Eras*. London. http://pubs.iied.org/pdfs/10613IIED.

pdf acc. May 18, 2020; T. Nefedova (2001) 'Blagoustroistvo gorodov i selskoi mestnosti. Derevnia v gorode', in T. Nefedova, G. P. M. Polyan and A. I. Treivish (eds.) *Gorod i derevnya v Evropeiskoi Rossii: Sto let peremen.* Moscow: OGI, 400–413.

6 Geoffrey Hosking (1997) *Russia: People and Empire, 1552–1917.* Cambridge: Harvard University Press.

7 S. Boylan (1996) 'Organized crime and corruption in Russia: Implications for U.S. and international law', *Fordham International Law Journal*, 19:5, 1999–2027.

8 Federal Service for State Registration. Cadastre and Cartography. https://rosreestr. ru/site/activity/gosudarstvennoe-upravlenie-v-sfere-ispolzovaniya-i-okhrany-zemel/ gosudarstvennyy-monitoring-zemel/sostoyanie-zemel-rossii/gosudarstvennyy-natsionalnyy-doklad-o-sostoyanii-i-ispolzovanii-zemel-v-rossiyskoy-federatsii/ acc. May 18, 2020.

9 Religious Belief and National Belonging in Central and Eastern Europe. www. pewforum.org/2017/05/10/religious-belief-and-national-belonging-in-central-and-eastern-europe/ acc. May 18, 2020.

10 *Putin's Russia: How It Rose, How It Is Maintained, and How It Might End.* Edited by Leon Aron. Washington, DC: American Enterprise Institute, 2015.

11 The World Factbook – Central Intelligence Agency. www.cia.gov/library/publi cations/the-world-factbook/geos/rs.html acc. May 18, 2020.

12 Employment and Unemployment in the Russian Federation in February 2020. https://gks.ru/bgd/free/B04_03/IssWWW.exe/Stg/d05/53.htm acc. May 18, 2020.

13 Federal State Statistics Service. www.gks.ru/folder/313/document/72529 acc. May 18, 2021.

14 Causes of Mortality in Russia. Demoscope. www.demoscope.ru/weekly/2020/ 0849/barom04.php acc. May 18, 2021.

15 Comprehensive Monitoring of the Living Conditions of the Population. www. gks.ru/free_doc/new_site/KOUZ18/index.html acc. May 18, 2021.

16 The Economist Intelligence Unit. Global Health Care. https://eiuperspectives. economist.com/sites/default/files/Globalaccesstohealthcare-3.pdf acc. May 18, 2021.

17 The Economist Intelligence Unit. The Quality of Life Index 2013. www.economist. com/news/2012/11/21/the-lottery-of-life acc. May 18, 2021.

2 History

2.1 Funeral arrangements and cemeteries in the Russian Empire (1721–1917)

Until the end of the 17th century, Orthodox Church parishes had managed funerals and funeral infrastructure as a whole in Russia. Church servants dug graves and buried Orthodox Christians in small graveyards. They also produced all of the funeral's hardware, including coffins and wooden crosses. Such graveyards were located near the church and usually reached about 2–3 acres in size. Graveyards were always overcrowded and had no individual plots or gravemarkers. We find evidence of the funeral arrangements in rare records of foreign guests of Russia from this time. For example, evidence can be found in the records of the English ambassador Charles Howard, Earl of Carlisle, who visited Moscow in the 1760s, or in the diary entries of Samuel Collins, who was the court physician of Tsar Alexei Mikhailovich (17th century).[1] They described a poor state of affairs of the Orthodox graveyards – of course, there was no state legislative regulation of graveyards and funerals. However, the overall situation with funerals and graveyards was very similar to any other European country in the same period.

The first attempts to regulate graveyards (but not funeral arrangements) were made in the 17th century. In 1657, during the plague in Moscow, the Urban Development Code forbade burials on the territory of the Moscow Kremlin. Since this time, all new graveyards have been established outside the Kremlin wall. The new decree of Tsar Fedor Alekseevich on April 7, 1682, contained several requirements for determining the boundaries of graveyards to facilitate property disputes between church and landlords. However, these requirements were not complied with.

Churchyards remained overcrowded and in disrepair. For example, on April 10, 1746, half a century after a decree by Tsar Fedor Alekseevich, Empress Elizabeth Petrovna noted that Kalinin and Voznesenie cemeteries

DOI: 10.4324/9781003153672-2

in St. Petersburg were filled up and emitted the stench of dead bodies.[2] Under Empress Catherine II at the end of the 18th century, and due to the lack of urban land and the threat of infection, the principles for the sanitary management of urban cemeteries were legally approved for the first time in the history of Russia.[3] These requirements exclusively concerned new cemeteries and, for a long time, were applied only to St. Petersburg and Moscow. The first large cemeteries outside the city boundaries were opened in Moscow in 1771: Vvedensky, Kalitnikovskoe, Vagankovskoe, Rogozhskoe, and Preobrazhenskoe cemeteries. These cemeteries were rather big compared with familiar churchyards and were divided into individual and family plots. They also had initial architectural planning. However, these cemeteries remained under the control of the Church.

In the 18th century, new cemeteries started to include unique places for nobles, clergy, and merchants. Some upper classes preferred to be buried in specific cemeteries. For example, merchants chose the Novodevichy Cemetery; scientists and artists preferred the Vvedensky Cemetery. Despite the positive funeral trends, these cemeteries were still rather conservative and religious. There were no 'cemetery garden' projects, large civil projects, or national necropolises as it happened in England with the Highgate Cemetery, for instance.

The vast majority of burials in the Russian Empire took place in graveyards. Until the end of the 19th century, graveyards and cemeteries were poorly regulated. There was no system of centrally collated statistics or bureaucratic oversight or central funding. Burials were registered in the church records. The burial plots were distributed by the local community; the maintenance of even large cemeteries was performed with the money of local parishioners. We may indicate it as a *moral economy*.[4] Thus, the maintenance of cemeteries became a 'common good' for the wide range of people associated with this cemetery. This fact is also confirmed by descriptions of the rural graveyards compiled at the behest of Grand Duke Nikolai Mikhailovich. At the turn of the 19th century, the Grand Duke asked church ministers to compile brief descriptions of all the graveyards and cemeteries. Unfortunately, work on the *Russian Provincial Necropolis* by Grant Duke Nikolai was interrupted by World War I. However, some of the collected data remains.[5]

According to this source, most of the churchyards in imperial Russia did not contain memorial signs or included just traditional wooden crosses. Stone monuments were rare for the vast majority of cemeteries. The burial plots were maintained for no more than a hundred years; then the grave was re-used. Descriptions by an unknown priest also include indications of the poor condition of cemeteries, constant looting of burial grounds, and the resale of monuments. For example, the priest from the city of Tula wrote that his churchyard 'is partly slaughtered by cattle, partly is seized under noble houses'.[6]

The complex regulating legislation of cemeteries was adopted in 1889. The law was called the 'Medical Regulations' (*Vrachebnyi Ukaz*). This act forbade the use of old burials for arable land, established a minimum distance from the cemetery to housing, and introduced normative regulations of some sanitary standards. Moreover, 'Medical Regulations' confirmed the ban on opening private cemeteries: religious and national communities were made responsible for arranging burial plots, and all cemeteries services were to be carried out by special funeral artels, which were cooperative associations of craftsmen living and working together. At this time, there were already many private cemeteries opened in Europe and the USA.

If the situation with cemeteries is clear, then what was happening with the organization of the funeral arrangements in the Russian Empire? Generally, as with burial places, funerals were regulated by the Church and a group of parishioners at each church. They arranged funerals and managed the cemetery, including digging the grave and so forth. Besides this church management, there still were opportunities for private funeral services including the production and sale of coffins and funeral hardware.

There was a very clear gradation of funeral arrangements, which depended on the social status of the deceased. There were five grades, with extreme differences between grades. For example, in St. Petersburg first-class funerals cost ₽950, while the monthly salary of a skilled worker at the beginning of the century amounted to ₽40–50 a month. The funeral for the fifth category cost ₽10. If a person died without funds for a funeral, the cost was generally met by friends and relatives.[7] Most of this amount was spent on organizing a procession. As a rule, the funeral procession included the rental of a hearse, horses in mourning pompoms, and people who carried torches. The number of horses and people in the procession depended on the status of the funeral. Money was also spent on the decoration of the coffin, house, and church where the farewell took place. For example, in March 1810, the Siberian merchant of the 3rd Guild Nikolai Ivanovich Popov died in Omsk. The report on his funeral reveals such burial expenses as the purchase of a coffin; candles and incense; bricks for laying in the grave; people who carried the coffin and dug a grave; canvas, braid, and ribbons; and psalm readers.[8] According to various archival data, a significant portion of expenditure was constituted by the price of the coffin and undertaker services. The average cost of a coffin was ₽2. Six hearse horses for the ceremony cost ₽12. Sixteen torchlights for the procession will cost almost ₽10,60 each.

Of course, traditional (peasant) Russian funerals were very different from the described. They also included a procession through the village on a cart with a horse. Special weepers participated in this kind of funeral, and a special funeral dinner was included. This dinner was often held at the burial plot. Such funerals were held on their own without the involvement of any funeral professionals. The coffin was made by a local carpenter as well as the other necessary accessories. This kind of organization was representative of 80 percent of the funerals in the Russian Empire.[9]

From the beginning of the 19th century, undertakers, coffin makers, and funeral companies began to appear in the big cities of the Russian Empire. As in Europe, most of them were originally furniture makers or carpenters and gradually became a separate profession.[10] Their revenue was not very high and the work was regarded as low status. Most businesses were small: funeral home staff consisted of several people, and necessary additional employees were hired as needed (what we call now 'freelance'). This work is well documented. For example, in 1895 the St. Petersburg journalist Nikolay Zhivotov worked for several days as an undertaker and torchbearer and wrote a book about his experience.[11] From his notes, we learn that most of these workers came from the lower social class: they scraped by on casual earnings and eked out an impoverished existence. By the beginning of the 20th century, around 70 funeral homes were in operation. Taking into account the mortality rates, we can say that one bureau executed about 20 funerals per month. However, we do not know about the earning power of the business and the average cost of the funeral. However, we can tell that the total profit was not high.

The funeral industry lagged far behind the industry in the Western world, where at the start of the 20th century, coffin production factories were already successfully operating and the first professional associations appeared.

During the years 1890–1900 there were several proposals to create crematoria in the Russian Empire, but they did not find practical support.[12] By the time of the October Revolution, there was not a single crematorium in the Russian Empire, except for a small military crematorium in Vladivostok for subjects of the Japanese Empire who died during the Russian-Japanese War (1905). In 1909, a commission specially created by the Holy Synod analyzed this ritual and issued a note on the burning of corpses from an Orthodox Church point of view: 'the Christian Orthodox Church never knew and does not recognize any other form of disposal of the dead bodies other than burial to the ground'. At the same time, the authorities of the Russian empire were not against the construction of crematoria. The main problem was the position of the Orthodox Church.[13]

Summary

- Funeral arrangements and all funeral infrastructure were under the control of the Church;

- Cemeteries were maintained by the local church community on the principles of 'moral economy';
- Private funeral business was developed only in big cities and it was a small urban craft production.

2.2 Funeral changes in early USSR (1917–1945)

The October Revolution (1917) profoundly influenced funeral organization. The new government decided to change the old Tsarist regime radically and started the secularization and nationalization of private property. One of the first documents adopted by the new government was the decree 'About Land' October 26 (November 8) in 1917. This decree transferred all monastery and church lands to the management of the Soviets' peasant deputies. Church lands included not only monasteries, temples, and outbuildings but also cemeteries, which were essentially nationalized under this decree. The Soviet state began to control cemeteries. Any payment for the graves was canceled, and Soviet people could now be buried in any cemetery, not just in their parish.

The decree 'On cemeteries and funerals', passed in December 1918, abolished the ranks of burial, and the Orthodox Church and private companies were removed from funeral affairs. All private funeral homes were nationalized and transferred to local councils from February 1, 1919. Thus, the new Soviet state nationalized the funeral infrastructure and established a state monopoly by banning a private funeral business. These decisions had a practical goal: the creation of a new Soviet ritual as a part of the 'New Soviet Man' project.[14] However, quite quickly, the nationalization of the funeral infrastructure had faced many economic and management problems. Maintenance of infrastructure required a variety of resources, both financial and human, which did not materialize. The Civil War of 1917–1922 mobilized employees of former funeral homes and cemeteries into the Red Army, and no funds were allocated for the organization of funerals.[15] Besides, previous rate payments to the general office of the cemetery from parishioners ceased; church parishes were closed.

As a result, cemeteries and the rest of the funeral infrastructure quickly fell into serious crisis. According to the report of Public Utilities Workers in September 1920: 'Cemeteries were in trouble, roads were not cleared, bridges were broken, wooden fences needed repair'; 'by that time the cemeteries were in a terrible situation, over 200 corpses were not buried and lay frozen on the ground'.[16] There was a lack of resources for the funerals in all cities – workers and even coffins were in a short supply: 'The problem of cemetery overcrowding has always existed, but in 1919–1920 this factor, together with the problems of logistics and supply – the absence of coffins, horses, vehicles, shovels and crowbars, grave diggers – significantly aggravated the funeral crisis in the city'. In an attempt to overcome this crisis, utilities began to bury bodies in mass graves. According to archival data, the maximum capacity of large Moscow cemeteries, 98 percent of the total number of burials, ranged from 100 to 500 bodies, subject to burial in mass graves. In fact, this meant that there was only enough space in these cemeteries to bury the corpses that had already accumulated in the hospitals and morgues of the city by the spring of 1919.[17]

Cemeteries were declining even against the backdrop of the economic crisis: people used old wooden crosses for heating, and monuments for household needs, and used the cemetery for grazing. In 1923, the funeral subdivision of the Department for the Improvement of Housing and Public Utilities was openly forced to admit that the cemeteries had become entirely unusable.

This crisis prompted the Main Directorate of Public Utilities to develop a new decree on funeral affairs to urgently reverse nationalization. Cooperatives and private citizens were given the right to organize funeral fraternities, funeral homes, and shops selling funeral supplies. This decree became possible within the framework of the New Economic Policy (1921–1928), during which there were softening conditions for private economic relations. It yielded some short-term results, and the funeral crisis was overcome although the maintenance of cemeteries remained an unresolved issue. However, the return of private business to the funeral arrangements was quickly curtailed along with the end of the New Economic Policy in 1928. Funeral homes returned to the status of being local public utilities, part of an extensive communal infrastructure along with bathhouses, landfills, and slaughterhouses.

Utilities took the funeral homes back without much enthusiasm. Cemeteries and funerals were continually being transferred from one public authority to another in an attempt to reduce maintenance costs. The constant bureaucratic transfer from one department to another meant that in practice funeral arrangements lacked any formal state oversight. For example, from 1928 in the cities of the RSFSR, there were 3276 public enterprises, and only 10 of them belonged to funeral arrangements. Due to the constant redeployment of the funeral function from one communal organization to another, municipal services could not fulfill their duties.

In the late 1920s, utilities returned to the pre-revolutionary funeral payment model. They introduced funeral classes and set tariffs. It was a simplified tariff schedule, including three classes. Due to rapid inflation, it makes no sense to cite specific figures, and I shall only note that they were not high. However, this did not produce any changes. Until the end of the 1930s, the funeral organization remained in a crisis state and experienced constant problems with resources. For example, in the reference book for 1931 *All Novosibirsk*, the funeral state department is stated as the only one in the entire city. A similar situation is recorded in all cities of the USSR.

The crisis in funerary organization was compounded by a program of active destruction by the Soviet government. During the anti-religious campaign, most church necropolises were looted and closed. As early as 1925, bronze and marble sculptural details began to be admitted to the museum of the Old Petersburg Society from the Smolensk Cemetery of Petersburg. Ancient tombstones were sent for sale as a building material or were reused as monuments by the new 'middle class' of Soviet society. A quarter of the houses for the Soviet elite were built on the site of the Dorogomilovsky Cemetery. An estimated 1000 cemeteries were destroyed in the time of the USSR, and more than a million graves were lost. Former cemeteries were closed and turned into city parks and squares. In Nizhny Novgorod, the Kulibin Park was made from the Peter and Paul Cemetery, and the former Pechersk Cemetery, they made a square for walking. Similar grave parks arose throughout the Soviet Union, in Kazan, Perm, and Novosibirsk.

2.3 Cremation in early USSR (1917–1945)

For the early Soviet ideologists, cremation seemed to be the right way of burial for a new Soviet man. Cremation was associated with ideas of progress, purity, technologies, and anticlericalism: 'Side by side with a car, tractor, and electrification – make way for cremation'.[18] Cremation was to replace traditional Orthodox below-ground burial and, more than that, close the cemeteries. Cremation was very actively promoted in the newspapers. However, the implementation of the project was more complicated than propaganda. The project of Soviet crematoria failed for a number of reasons that we will consider.

Soviet authorities tried to organize the first crematorium in 1919 in Petrograd, but the project was delayed for a year due to the Civil War. The crematorium was opened in the boiler room of the former baths on Vasilyevsky Island, 14th line, house 95–97. Its basis was the regenerative cremation furnace 'Metallurgist' designed by Professor V.N. Lipin. This crematorium was working for a little over two months before it was closed: the 'Metallurgist' cremation furnace broke down constantly, and the process involved significant fuel consumption, taking up to 300 kilograms of firewood per cremation.

A crematorium was erected at the site of the former cemetery of the Donskoy Monastery in Moscow in 1927, and the design project of crematoria for each Soviet city was prepared. Learning from the unsuccessful experience of using the cremation furnace 'Metallurgist' in the St. Petersburg crematorium, for the Donskoy Crematorium, the furnace was ordered in

Germany. The crematorium was built in the style of Soviet constructivism. Inside was an organ dismantled from an Anglican church on Tverskaya Street, Moscow. This crematorium was cremating not only ordinary people but also honored members of the party, government, and other Soviets celebrities, such as Vladimir Mayakovsky, Maxim Gorky, Valery Chkalov, S. Kirov, V. Kuybyshev, S. Ordzhonikidze, A. Bogdanov, and many others.

With the opening of the Donskoy Crematorium, newspaper pages were filled with articles and feuilletons glorifying cremation as a new and, most crucially, ideologically correct way to conduct the funeral of a Soviet man. The Society for the Development of the Idea of Cremation in the RSFSR was established in 1927, working in close cooperation with the Union of Militant Atheists. In 1932 the society was transformed into the All-Russian Cremation Society.

The columbarium of the Donskoy Cemetery, located next to the crematorium, is an excellent example of the early attempts of the Soviet government to construct a unique culture of death. Thousands of unique urns, epitaphs, and designs of unique niches are still in the columbarium. Many urns are homemade and represent an example of the unique Soviet funeral DIY culture.

Figure 2.1 Columbarium of the "Donskoy Crematorium". Our days.

Source: Photo by Sergey Prostakov.

Figure 2.1 (Continued)

Soviet ideologists dreamed of building a crematorium in literally every district of all Soviet cities. Stephen Kotkin notes, using the example of Magnitogorsk, that during the construction of the new Soviet cities, urban plans did not include cemeteries but they did stipulate crematoria.[19] However, despite active propaganda, Soviet citizens were reluctant to use cremation services: they were expensive, cremators often broke down, and there continued to be a preference for earth burial. By the 1930s, Soviet leaders had begun to lose interest in cremation as an effective ideological weapon.

Summary

- By the beginning of World War II, a private funeral business in the USSR was prohibited and the state took over responsibility.
- However, centralized government funding was not then provided to continue to provide those services.
- A significant number of cemeteries was physically destroyed or passed into an ownerless status; funeral homes were relocated to public services; the production of coffins and funeral accessories was not established.

- Soviet utilities began to neglect their funeral and cemetery maintenance responsibilities due to the lack of professional and financial resources.
- The cremation project failed.

2.4 National necropolises in the USSR

In the Russian Empire, nobles had preferred to be buried in unique cemeteries, creating the prototypes of national necropolises. Such cemeteries were based on the territory of monasteries, and some of them have survived until the present day, for example, Novodevichy Cemetery or the Donskoy Necropolis. As I have noted, these were different from typical Russian cemeteries, first of all, because of the presence of memorial sculpture.

In the Soviet Union, no projects were undertaken to build individual memorials. The party elite preferred cremation and then burial in Red Square, setting the urn directly into the wall. The Kremlin necropolis also incorporates several mass graves, which were used extensively in the 1920s. However, Nikita Khrushchev and party associates Anastas Mikoyan and Nikolai Podgorny were buried in the Novodevichy Cemetery. In total, more than 400 people rest in the necropolis, and the latest buried was the Secretary-General of the CPSU Central Committee Konstantin Chernenko (1985).

A decision about a national Pantheon was made in 1953 by the resolution of the Council of Ministers of the USSR. The Pantheon was designed as 'a monument to the eternal glory of the great people of the Soviet country'. It was planned to transfer the remains of Vladimir Lenin and Joseph Stalin, as well as 'the remains of prominent figures of the Communist Party and the Soviet state, buried near the Kremlin wall'. However, construction works were stopped after the 20th Congress of the CPSU, where Nikita Khrushchev announced the struggle against the personality cult of Stalin.[20]

The Soviet elite favored burial in the central cemeteries of Soviet cities. For example, Vvedensky Cemetery has become a cemetery for scientists and artists.

2.5 Funerals in the post-war USSR (1945–1960)

World War II losses of the Soviet Union from all related causes were about 27 million people, both civilian and military.[21] World War II had a serious impact on the culture of death in the Soviet Union: in every family there was someone who died in the war. War and fallen soldiers became a principal emphasis in family mourning.

World War II caused massive damage that included the destruction of cemeteries. Rebuilding effort was focused on housing, sewage, and social infrastructure. In this context, cemeteries and morgues were not the highest priority. There was continuity in the failure of episodic attempts made by the Soviet authorities to stabilize the funeral arrangements

From the late 1930s, funerals had passed into the zone of responsibility of the Soviet citizens themselves. It had become largely impossible to purchase monuments, coffins, wreaths, or to order hearses through official agents of public utilities. Each family secured a coffin, prepared the burial plot, and installed and manufactured monuments for themselves. Now we would call it 'DIY'. Independent manufacturing of funeral accessories from improvised materials was widespread. The tomb monuments were made from pipe scraps, old mechanical parts, metal ceilings, etc. Old pre-revolutionary gravestones were polished and used for the new commemorative signs. Often fences, monuments, and coffins were made in the carpentry shops of enterprises where the deceased worked. As the cultural researcher Pavel Kudyukin notes, 'soviet life from a cradle to the grave' entirely depended on the resources that were available where a person worked.[22] It was this diversion of work resources that compensated for the market deficit of the Soviet economy and funeral services, in particular, providing material resources for the funeral.

In the post-war years, the USSR had an extensive network of shadow artisanal economies that produced all the necessary material resources for the funeral realm. The informal funeral economy functioned in the same way as other services:

> Ordinary people unable to satisfy their needs in the state economy of scarcity had to have recourse to blat, the mutual exchange of goods and services. This might be hierarchical or horizontal: through a patron with good access to official sources or through a friend able to acquire foreign goods or with a link to the underground economy, where 'illegal' goods were obtainable. Blat occupied a shadowy area between the gift economy, the barter economy and the market economy. It inevitably entailed trusting people one would not normally trust – exemplifying another variant of 'forced trust'.[23]

'Grassroots' cooperation existed in the USSR in the 1950s and compensated for the constant shortage of consumer goods in the Soviet Union. It should be noted that bricolage in funeral arrangements was supported by the official authorities, who believed that the iron, concrete, and wood were better directed to industrial goals and the Cold War but not for funerals. It is curious and indicative that the Soviet government encouraged such homemade practices. Soviet architects, such as Aleksandr Chaldymov, even developed various designs of wooden monuments.[24] As implied, Soviet citizens had to make them on their own. Moreover, in the projects under development of such monuments, architects reached out for the traditional peasant forms of Russian funeral crosses.[25]

A similar situation occurred with cemeteries, which were not formally managed. Grave plots were not fixed by law, and so people began to set up fences as material evidence of their rights to the grave. It is crucial to note that new graves began to appear at cemeteries that had been destroyed during the war. These burials were in contravention of formal regulations requiring cemeteries to comply with certain sanitary standards, be officially registered, and have a development plan. An estimated 90 percent of the cemeteries in the post-war period emerged spontaneously. Often, burial plots were chosen in the immediate vicinity of residential buildings and/ or along the borders of other infrastructural facilities. At the same time, the cemetery eradication program continued in the 1950s and 1960s: Soviet cities, being under active construction, demanded free spaces.

The Soviet post-war funeral industry, if we may call it 'industry', failed not only in organizing the production of funeral hardware but even in creating a special funeral transport. Trucks and buses were commonly used as hearses.[26] Soviet buses (like PAZ and YerAZ) were adapted for the needs of funeral arrangements: a special place for the coffin was added to the car interior, or a door was fitted in the luggage compartment of the truck. Using

Figure 2.2 A coffin with a deceased and a DIY gravestone are being taken by truck to the cemetery. Unknown author.

Source: Photo from the author's own collection.

trucks as funeral cars was logical in the Soviet consumption culture. The USSR car culture was in its infancy, while the Soviet factories produced buses and trucks more than any other country in the world.[27] The need for such vehicles was also determined by the poor quality of roads and long distances between infrastructural objects.

Of course, large-scale projects also took place. For example, the only mortuary in the USSR was built in 1958 in the small city of Volzhsky, near Stalingrad. This building was intended for mourning ceremonies. The mortuary, by an unknown architect, was built in the tradition of Stalinist architecture and is vaguely reminiscent of an ancient temple. In 1974, 'Cemetery No. 1' officially closed, and there was no longer a need for a huge mortuary. No documents on the construction of the mortuary in Volzhsky have been preserved, and this mortuary has since been destroyed.

Thus, all of these factors influenced the institutional consolidation of the post-war Soviet 'DIY' funeral culture. The peasant population, which moved to the cities, did not perceive the funeral as a market service. In theory, maintenance as well as development of communal infrastructure was one of the social obligations of the state. In reality, the funeral – as well as everything related to funeral infrastructure – was a matter of collective participation and mutual assistance, but not a market good or social service. Similar practices of grassroots self-organization characterized traditional Russian culture in general. This culture did not reflect market relations in the Western sense. To some extent, a regression occurred: the organization of the funeral in the USSR ceased to become a market good or public service but evolved into an element of the grassroots cultural life.

2.6 Funerals in the late Soviet times (1960–1991)

In the 1970s, Soviet authorities returned to the issue of funeral arrangements. At this time, new efforts were made to regulate funeral activities. Soviet authorities were developing funeral shops and introducing the production and sale of monuments but the USSR was experiencing a shortage of goods. which meant that the population still compensated through recourse to DIY strategies. Therefore, in many ways, state attempts to develop the funeral sphere were superficial and issues remained unresolved.

The first post-war attempt to regulate cemeteries was taken in 1960. The chief sanitary inspector of the USSR M. Nikitin introduced the document 'Sanitary Rules for the Construction and Maintenance of Cemeteries' under No. 343–60. This document determined general rules for the operation of cemeteries including the depth and width of graves and location with respect to residential areas. This short document did not vary much from the previous document adopted in 1948. These sanitary requirements were

Figure 2.3 The funeral in the new city quarter. Moscow 1970s. Unknown author.

Source: Photo from the author's own collection.

the only regulatory paper governing the operation and principles of the construction of the Soviet cemetery. However, the document did not contain any instructions on the procedure for interaction between authorities or on monitoring the implementation of these recommendations.

In 1977, the first serious projects for the reconstruction of the funeral sphere in the USSR appeared. 'Sanitary rules for the construction and maintenance of cemeteries' (No. 1600–77) were more significant than previous regulations and included the requirements of architectural projects for cemeteries. In addition, the instruction 'Procedure for the funeral and the maintenance of cemeteries in the RSFSR' by the Ministry of Housing and Communal Services was issued in 1979. The instructions proposed a new type of the Soviet necropolis project. This project suggested the installation of a unique building for public mourning, gardens, as well as some instructions for funerals. The instructions permitted the 'direct provision of services to citizens and the sale of funeral supplies', to be 'operated by specialized salons-shops of specialized public services'. It was the first Soviet document aimed at centralizing the funeral and defining how funeral homes should operate, what infrastructure should be included, and how 'basic Soviet funerals' should take place. The plan was to provide numerous buildings for memorial services, open funerary stores, and funeral director services. Broadly constructed, the Soviet state was revolving around the idea of a unified regulation of the funeral.

However, as one would expect, ambitious plans were not realized except for the construction of several new crematoria. In 20 years (1970–1990), eight new crematoria were built: Nikolo-Arkhangelsky in Moscow in 1972, in Leningrad in 1973, Yekaterinburg in 1982, and two more in Moscow in 1987 and 1988. Crematoria were also built in Kiev (1975), Minsk (1986), and Tbilisi (1974). These projects were delivered in the Soviet futuristic style and also incorporated memorial parks and unique rooms for mourning events. All of them were owned by the state.

The following changes occurred in the late 1980s: on February 5, 1987, a special decree of the Presidium of the Supreme Soviet of the USSR allowed the creation of private trade and cooperatives in the USSR. These documents influenced only the most general principles of the market economy, and, of course, there was nothing about the funeral business in particular. However, the very possibility of legal provision of private services was directly related to the funeral service: in the same year, the first 'Crystal' funeral services cooperative was founded in Moscow.

Based on the Soviet garage economy, numerous funeral cooperatives and funeral service companies started appearing in the cities. So, for instance, in Moscow in the first five years after cooperatives started, the number of such companies increased by several times. The previously described system of shadow/handicraft funeral hardware production served as the material base for the creation and development of such cooperatives. The first legal private structures began to appear on the basis of numerous factories, garage societies, carpentry workshops, which for decades were producing funeral accessories for the needs of the population. They were making coffins, fences, monuments, and other funeral accessories. Many cooperatives emerged not only grounding on informal production in private garages but also in reliance on rapidly decaying Soviet industrial infrastructure. The shadow production of funeral accessories and funeral services were legalized.

Despite the legalization of market relations, funeral infrastructure was still kept in the hands of the state (councils/municipalities): funeral cooperatives were only allowed to conduct funerals, as well as to sell funeral paraphernalia. Thus, local authorities still had to maintain a costly expanding infrastructure without the necessary funding. However, even the opportunity to create private funeral companies did not significantly reform the funeral sphere and did not lead either to its rapid development or to an increase in the quality of services. The cemeteries remained in an ownerless status, and the products of the funeral services market, although covering the shortage of goods, still did not meet the minimum quality standards.

The historical aspect is crucial for further understanding of the funeral organization in modern Russia. Over many decades, a quite specific area of economic and cultural activity developed in the USSR, largely outside the control of the state.

By the time of the collapse of the USSR in 1991, the condition of funeral affairs had the following features:

- The vast majority of cemeteries sat outside any formal legal framework: it remains the case that the exact number of burials and their location are not known. There is no funding for systematic maintenance or management.
- Funeral infrastructure and the funeral industry remained underdeveloped: a market in the production of funeral accessories and, in particular, hearses had not been established.
- There were no developed regulatory framework and regulatory bodies.
- There was no system of statistics and accounting.
- Soviet funeral culture was formed as a 'DIY culture'.

Notes

1　S. Collins (1671/2008) *The Present State of Russia*. Edited by M. Poe. London: Iowa Research Online.
2　N. Pavlenko (2005). *Elizaveta Petrovna: V krugu muz i favoritov*. Moscow: AST, 122.
3　This happened at the same time with the European transfer of cemeteries outside the city – for example, in Paris, Vienna, Milan and so on. H. Mytum (2003) 'The social history of the European cemetery', in C. D. Bryant (ed.) *Handbook of Death and Dying*, Vol. 2. Thousand Oaks: Sage, 801–810.
4　J. C. Scott (1977) *The Moral Economy of the Peasant: Rebellion and Subsistence in Southeast Asia*. New Haven, CT: Yale University Press; S. K. Wegren (2005) *The Moral Economy Reconsidered: Russia's Search for Agrarian Capitalism*. New York: Palgrave Macmillan; A. Sokolova (2019) 'Soviet funeral services: From moral economy to social welfare and back', *Revolutionary Russia*, 32:2, 251–271.
5　*Russian Provincial Necropolis/Comp. V.V. Sheremetevsky*. Reprint edition of 1914. St. Petersburg: Alfaret, 2006, 1028.
6　*Russian Provincial Necropolis/Comp. V.V. Sheremetevsky*. Reprint edition of 1914. St. Petersburg: Alfaret, 2006, 724.
7　M. Logunova (2010) 'Traurnyj ceremonial v Rossijskoj imperii', *Vlast*, 3, 3–13.
8　K. Gizieva (2016) 'Gorodskoj pogrebal'nyj obrjad vtoroj poloviny xix – nachala HH veka (na primere Omska)', *Manuskript*, 12:2, 74.
9　M. Logunova (2017) 'Pechal'nye ritualy imperatorskoj Rossii', *Centrpoligraf*, 317.
10　D. H. Kaiser (1992) 'Death and dying in early modern Russia', in N. S. Kollman (ed.) *Major Problems in Early Modern Russian History*. London: Garland, 217–258.
11　N. Zhivotov (1895) *Among the Torches Men: Six Days in the Role of a Torch Bearer*. Izd. Den: Saint-Petersburg.

12 Pravdzik B. Krematsiya [Cremation]. SPb.: Tipo-litografiya, fototipiya of V. I. Schtain, 1892. 45.

13 Doklad komissii o narodnom zdravii po zakonoproektu ob ustroistve kladbishch i krematoriev, o pogrebenii i registratsii umershikh [The report of the Commission on the people's health on the draft law on the structure of cemeteries and crematoria, burial, and registration of deaths]: Prilozheniya k stenograficheskim otchetam Gosudarstvennoi dumy. Vol. 6 (No. 556–643). Chetvertyi sozyv, 1913–1914 gg. Sessiya vtoraya [Annexes to the verbatim records of the State Duma. Vol. 6 (No. 556–643). The fourth convocation, 1913–1914 Session two]. SPb.: Gosudarstvennaya typografia, No. 579.

14 C. Merridale (2002) *Night of Stone: Death and Memory in Twentieth-Century Russia*. Harmsworth: Penguin Books; J. McDowell, J. (1974) 'Soviet civil ceremonies', *Journal for the Scientific Study of Religion*, 13:3, 265–279; C. A. P. Binns (1979) 'The changing face of power: Revolution and accommodation in the development of the Soviet ceremonial system. Part I', *Man* (New series), 14, 585–606; C. A. P. Binns (1980) 'The changing face of power: Revolution and accommodation in the development of the Soviet ceremonial system. Part II', *Man* (New series), 15, 170–187.

15 A. D. Sokolova (2018) 'Novii mir i staraja smert: sudba kladbisch v sovetskikh gorogakh 1920–1930h godov' [New world and the old death: The fate of cemeteries in the Soviet cities of the 1920s–1930s], *Neprikosnovennyi zapas*, 117:1, 74–94; A. D. Sokolova (2013) '"Nel'zia, nel'zia novykh liudei khoronit' po-staromu!" Evoliutsiia pokhoronnogo obriada v Sovetskoi Rossii ["It is impossible, it is impossible to bury new people in the old way!" Evolution of the funeral rite in Soviet Russia], *Otechest vennye zapiski*, 5:56, 191–208.

16 I. Orlov (2015) *Kommunal'naia strana. Stanovlenie sovetskogo zhilishchnokom munal'nogo khoziaistva (1917–1941)*. Moscow: HSE University Press.

17 S. Mokhov and A. Sokolova (2020) 'Broken infrastructure and soviet modernity: The funeral market in Russia', *Mortality*, 25:2, 232–248.

18 G. Barthel (1925) 'K postroike v Moskve pervogo v SSSR krematoriya' [Construction in Moscow of the first Soviet crematorium], *Kommunal'noe khozyaistvo* [Communal Economy], 23, 25–37.

19 S. Kotkin (1997) *Magnetic Mountain: Stalinism as a Civilization*. Oakland, CA: University of California Press.

20 XX Congress of the CPSU. Verbatim report. Moscow, 1956.

21 G. F. Krivosheev (1997) *Soviet Casualties and Combat Losses in the Twentieth Century*. Barnsley: Greenhill Books, 85.

22 P. Kudukin (2012) '"Proizvodstvennaja kvaziobshhina kak centr zhiznennogo mira", cited in The USSR: Life after Death (collection of articles ed. by I.V. Glushchenko, B.Y. Kagarlitsky, V.A. Kurennoj)', *Topos*, 1, 152–157.

23 S. Lovell, A. Rogachevskii and A. V. Ledeneva (eds.) (2000) *Bribery and Blat in Russia: Negotiating Reciprocity from the Early Modern Period to the 1990s*. London: Palgrave Macmillan, 312; A. V. Ledeneva (2008) '"Blat" and "guanxi": Informal practices in Russia and China', *Comparative Studies in Society and History*, 50:1, 118–144.

24 Iz stenogrammy soveshchaniia po problemam memorial'noi arkhitektury [From the transcript of the colloquium on the questions of memorial architecture]. 3–5 iiunia 1946 g. In Sovetskoe izobrazitel'noe iskusstvo i arkhitektura 60-kh–70-kh godov [Soviet representational art and architecture of the 1960–1970-s, A collection of articles]. Moscow, Nauka Publishers, 1979. Zadachi arkhitektorov v

dni Velikoi Otechestvennoi voiny. Materialy 10 plenuma pravleniia SSA SSSR 22–25 aprelia 1942 g. [Tasks of the architects in the days of the Great Patriotic War, Acts of 10th plenary session of the administration of the Union of Soviet Architects of the USSR]. Moscow, Gos. arhitekturnoe izd-vo Akademii arhitektury SSSR, 1942.

25 T. G. Malinina (2018) 'Cultural palimpsests: Their manifestation and reading in the architectural and artistic texts of the Soviet era', *Artikult*, 29:1, 75–96.

26 Of course, for the funerals of the party elite, a special hearse was used, modelled on Soviet luxury cars. But the hearses did not reach the general consumer.

27 L. H. Siegelbaum (2009) 'On the side: Car culture in the USSR, 1960s–1980s', *Technology and Culture*, 50:1, 1–23.

3 Funeral industry law and regulation framework

3.1 Federal and municipal authorities

Russian federalism is the basis of funeral regulation in contemporary Russia. There are four levels of regulation of the funeral industry:

- *Federal level frameworks general requirements.* The Ministry of Construction develops the general frameworks of the industry; the Federal Antimonopoly Service monitors cartel conspiracies and monopolies; the Ministry of Health regulates the work of morgues; the Sanitary-Epidemiological Service monitors the threat to public health and develops sanitary laws; the Prosecutor's Office ensures that there is no corruption. There are no supervisory and regulatory organizations that would control either the agents of the funeral market (such as Federal Trade Commission in the USA) or the functioning of the funeral infrastructure;
- *Regional, at the level of federal districts*;[1]
- *Regional, at the level of entities.* Management is the same as at the federal level, but only at the level of regional services – for example, the republican Ministry of Construction;
- *Municipal level.* The main role in regulating the funeral industry is assigned to municipalities. Local municipalities can adopt regulations and laws and create municipal funeral services. They are also required to maintain funeral infrastructure. According to federal law No. 8, 'On burial and funeral affairs', funerals are a public service. Therefore, municipalities are required to supervise and create necessary conditions for the provision of this service to citizens.

3.2 The private sector

According to the federal law No. 8, 'On burial and funeral affairs', the private sector provides funeral services including coaching, casketing, selling

DOI: 10.4324/9781003153672-3

funeral hardwares, and the burial service. All funeral infrastructure is state property (cemeteries), and the private sector can only create and maintain infrastructural facilities under public-private partnerships (mortuaries and crematoria).

The work of the private sector is regulated by three main government standards (GoSt). There are GoSt P 53107–2008 (funeral services, general terms); GoSt P 53099–2010 (crematorium services); GoSt P 54611–2011 (funeral services, requirements, and recommendations). In addition to this, there is SanPiN (sanitary rules and regulations) 2.1.2882–11, 'Hygienic requirements for the placement, construction and maintenance of cemeteries, buildings and structures for funeral purposes', which is important for the private sector too: this document sets out the requirements for the location of funeral homes in a residential area.

3.3 Death registration

Death registration is performed by private doctors, hospitals, and ambulances. If a person died at home or on the street, then the presence of the police is mandatory. A medical death certificate is required to obtain a state death certificate.

Registration of the fact of death is regulated by Article No. 66 of the Federal Law No. 323 *'On the Basics of Protecting the Health of Citizens in the Russian Federation'*, as well as by the Federal Law No. 143 *'On the Acts of Civil Status'* and the document of the Ministry of Health and Social Development №14–6/10/2–178 'On the procedure for issuing and filling out medical certificates of birth and death'.

In Russia, the place of death is not recorded – for example, a street, house, or hospital. Therefore, there is no general statistics on the place of death.

3.4 Funeral federal law

The first funeral law in contemporary Russia appeared in 1996, five years after the collapse of the USSR. It was federal law No. 8, 'On burial and funeral affairs' (*Федеральный закон 'О погребении и похоронном деле'*). It is a descriptive law and frames only basic recommendations. This document is still valid in Russia with minor amendments. Experts admit that this Federal Law is bad and outdated. Since 2012, a new federal law has been under development by The Ministry of Construction but has not yet been presented for public discussion (early 2020).

We can identify the following structure-forming principles in the law which frames Russian funeral arrangements:

- The funeral is a public good. A free funeral is guaranteed to every citizen of the Russian Federation. The state guarantees free paperwork, a burial plot in the cemetery, funeral services (storing the body in the morgue free for seven days, a basic coffin, and transportation of the body from mortuary to the cemetery).
- Free funeral services provided by municipalities. The federal law extended the status quo in funeral management that developed in Soviet times. The funeral market is a sphere of responsibility and regulation of the state with an emphasis on local municipalities. The federal law expressly states that local governments independently regulate and fund funeral activities in their own territory: 'The organization of a funeral is carried out by local governments. Burial and the provision of burial services are carried out by specialized funeral services established by local authorities' (Article 25.2). Local governments are therefore obliged to create specialized municipal funeral services (for example, to maintain a cemetery or transportation).
- Each Russian citizen can verbally or in writing form declare their wishes regarding the funeral arrangements, including a place for disposal.
- A person can be buried in a cemetery or cremated, and the ashes placed in a grave or columbarium. Storage at home is prohibited. Another disposal of the ashes may be only if the will of the deceased is expressed.
- The state either provides these services independently or reimburses expenditure. These compensations are established by each entity of the Federation independently.[2] By all means, it is worth admitting that the state's funeral services are of rather poor quality. The average cost of a funeral for which the state pays is about 7,000 ₽ ($90). Most people prefer to receive this money and make their own arrangements by the private sector.

If the citizen was a military or police officer, he is entitled to an extended list of free funeral services from the state. In this case, this person will receive an individual burial plot in the cemetery, a military music band, farewell in a specialized place, and the installation of a gravestone after the funeral. Similar rules apply to veterans of the military and other specialized services.

The arrangement of funerals of the lonely, destitute, unknown persons is also provided by the state (local authorities).

- The funeral infrastructure is fixed as state property and an object of state administration. Cemeteries, morgues, and crematoria are owned or managed by federal and municipal authorities.

- The federal law does not provide explicit definitions of funeral activities, funeral directors, definitions of professional competence of a funeral director, or the need for special education or training. The law does not spell out the procedure for official interaction between private and government funeral actors.
- The law and other normative acts do not specifically define the legal status of burial plots. The burial plots are not private property, but rather let on a long-term lease.

3.5 Regional legislation

As I noted, the main role in funeral industry regulation is assigned to municipalities. Therefore, the number of local regulatory documents is estimated at several thousands. Researchers note about 5000 different local regional acts (acts, rules, explanations, orders). These acts differ quite strongly from each other. In the vast majority of cases, they are entirely local. Municipal acts are adopted to create local utilities, maintain infrastructure, and define rules for the transport of dead bodies.

3.6 General requirements for funeral infrastructure

In Russia, there are several basic laws regarding funeral infrastructure, including sanitary requirements. The main one is the law number 2.1.2882–11 'Hygienic requirements for the placement, construction, and maintenance of cemeteries, buildings and structures for funeral purposes' (SanPin 2.1.2882–11), approved by the Decree of the Chief State Sanitary Doctor of the Russian Federation of June 28, 2011, No. 84.

The law requires that crematoria must be located at a distance of at least one kilometer from residential buildings; cemeteries of 20–40 hectares, 500m; cemeteries of 10–20 hectares, 300m; small cemeteries, 100m; and closed cemeteries, 50m. The zone of the objects is calculated from the cadastral border.

It is not possible to build near open water sources without an engineering and architectural plan. Cemeteries should be located well above the water table and have an adequate drainage system. It is recommended that the cemeteries have a driveway, a fence, and green spaces. These requirements in most cases are not necessarily complied with since there are no inspection bodies and the law can be interpreted in many ways.

3.7 Funeral paperwork

Documents for a funeral vary depending on the situation and method of disposal of the body. For example, paperwork relating to transportation in the morgue, crematorium, and cemetery is different. As a rule, all documents are executed by the funeral director. The only step where relatives of the deceased are required is when receiving a death certificate. Further, most commonly, relatives pass the passport of the deceased and the certificate to the funeral director, who is accountable for everything. As in most countries, the funeral director works a lot with documents.

Common documents required include:

- Death certificate, which is issued in a special authorities center on the basis of a medical certificate of death received in the morgue;
- Passport or ID of the supervisor of the funeral;
- A funeral services contract with the funeral agency; and
- A cashier's receipt issued by a funeral agency to compensate the sum insured.

Documents that a morgue requires in order to issue a medical death certificate:

- Passport or ID of the organizer of the funeral;
- Passport or identity card of the deceased; and
- Compulsory medical insurance policy for the deceased.

To pick up a body from a morgue, a set of documents is necessary:

- Passport or other identity document of the facilitator of the funeral; and
- Stamp death certificate, issued by special authorities center on the basis of a medical death certificate.

Documents for burial differ from those that are necessary for the registration of a burial in a new grave:

- Stamp certificate of death: issued by the special authorities center;
- Passport or ID of the funeral arranger;
- The services contract with the funeral service;
- Cashier's receipt;
- Passport of burial (certificate of burial). This is issued upon purchase of a family plot at the Moscow Department of Trade and Services; and
- Documents attesting to the kinship of the deceased with the existing burials in the event of burial in a family plot, for example, certificate of marriage, certificate of birth, court decision on adoption, court decision on recognition of kinship, etc.

If the body of the deceased is cremated, his relatives will need the following set of documents:

• Stamp death certificate issued by the special authorities center;
• Passport or ID of the funeral arranger; and
• An agreement on the cremation of the remains of the deceased and a receipt for the payment of crematorium services, issued by the crematorium where cremation is executed.

To pick up the urn with ashes from the crematorium, these documents are needed:

• Stamp death certificate: issued by the special authorities center;
• Passport or ID of the organizer of the funeral; and
• Cremation certificate issued by a crematorium after cremation.

For transportation between regions/countries, these documents are needed:

• Stamp certificate of death: issued by the special authorities center;
• Certificate from the sanitary-epidemiological service;
• Certificate of embalming the body, issued by morgue;
• Certificate on the tightness of the soldering of the zinc coffin;
• Certificate of the absence of foreign objects in the coffin; and
• Permission to transport the body to the destination point.

3.8 Legal contradictions

The normative framework established by federal law has been undermined by several regulatory conflicts and collisions. In outlining the legal framework, it is simpler to define the gaps and failings in the current system.

• There are no special requirements for establishing a private funeral company. Funeral directors have no exact definition. Anyone can set up a funeral company without special education and necessary licenses. The licensing system for funeral directors was canceled in 2003.
• Various types of funeral directors' activities fall under different taxation. For example, in general, funeral companies often use simplified taxation, as for 'household services'. At the same time, the sale of funeral supplies should be taxed like retail. However, there is no separation, and in reality, these rules are not complied with. Commonly funeral companies do not share their activities for tax surveillance.

- There is no state system of requirements for the quality of services and goods. Documents in this area are classified as recommendations. For example, the law requires that 'the transportation of the deceased to the place of burial should take place on a specialized transport. It is allowed to use another type of motor vehicle for the transportation of the deceased, except for motor vehicles used for the transportation of food raw materials and food products'.[3] The word 'specialized' does not indicate the technical features of such vehicles and measures. Another example: there is a resolution of the Chief State Sanitary Doctor of the Russian Federation dated June 28, 2011 No. 84 'On approval of SanPiN 2.1.2882–11. Hygienic requirements for the placement, construction and maintenance of cemeteries, buildings and structures for funeral purposes'. It implies that the basic requirements for the construction of cemeteries are advisory and are not strict requirements. There is also a national standard 'Domestic services. Funeral services. Terms and Definitions. GOST R 53107–2008', but it does not include any specific definitions and principles for classifying a service/product as a funeral service. According to this classifier, a funeral service stands for any service/product involved in the funeral procedure.
- There is no federal funeral statistics system. No official organization in Russia knows how many cemeteries operate in the country, how many people are buried in them, and, most importantly, who is buried where. The same applies to cremated ashes: there is no record of the location of the ashes. The state is not aware of what happens to a dead body after issuing it from a morgue. According to the requirements of the law, the body can be given out only to a relative or a responsible person, but it has not been established who and how should determine the degree of kinship between the deceased and the person who comes to pick up the body. Anyone can collect the body by presenting an ordinary passport. The lack of state statistics allows the funeral companies themselves to keep no record and avoid reporting: it is impossible to track how many funerals a particular funeral agency makes.

***

In summary, the legislative framework in the funeral sphere consolidated the institutional status quo of the Soviet model of public management. The following principle of separation of functions of the leading agents is confirmed. In essence, the state (local government, federal authorities, etc.) monopolizes the infrastructure, while private agents are allowed to organize the transportation of a dead body, the technical implementation of the burial itself, and the sale of funeral hardwares. Local municipalities need to maintain and develop the infrastructure entrusted to them, which, in fact, does not generate any substantial income. However, there are no tools and ways to control the agents of the funeral market. These conflicts lead to the development of the shadow market and many related practices, which will be discussed in the following.

Notes

1 There are eight federal districts in Russia: Central, Volga, Siberian, Southern, North-Western, Ural, North Caucasus, and Far Eastern.
2 The funeral financial support by state is carried out at the expense of the respective budgets following Articles 9, 10, 11 of this Federal Law.
3 Sanitary rules and norms 2.1.2882–11 'Hygienic requirements for the placement, operation and maintenance of cemeteries, buildings and infrastructure for funerals'.

4   Funeral directing industry

4.1 Changes in the funeral industry in contemporary Russia 1991–2020

First, I will outline the transformations in the funeral market over the past 30 years so that we can better understand the role of each group of actors and their functions. We can distinguish three main stages.

4.1.1 1991 to 2001

This is the period of a relatively rapid transition from the Soviet planned economy to a market economy. Private business was allowed in the funeral industry and dealt mainly with the production of accessories and different funeral services. At this point, the former cooperatives and artisanal production went through the process of legalization. During this period, all the authority was passed to the regions and municipalities within the Russian Federation, and each started to regulate the industry, including independent licensing of funeral operatives in a simplified notification form. The decision on issuing licenses was rendered by state institutions and professional regional funeral directors associations.

Major differences emerged between the regions at this stage. For example, in St. Petersburg, almost all small enterprises and former state-owned companies passed into the hands of several large public-private owners, and a monopoly was formed. At the same time, for example, in Kaluga the funeral business was utterly given to private agents and there were no municipal actors. During this period, the funeral market was developed quite freely and employment in the industry grew, including staff from related areas such as the former military and medicine.

DOI: 10.4324/9781003153672-4

4.1.2 2001 to 2014

The licensing system was canceled in 2001 at the instigation of the Federal Antimonopoly Service, in response to the closed nature of the market and the monopoly position of large public-private companies. This stage did not have a substantial impact on the funeral market in large cities since by this time, the market was already divided by different players at the regional level. The abolition of licensing had a greater impact in medium-sized cities and rural areas. The removal of a licensing framework meant that many smaller operatives re-appeared, and competition and corruption increased and it was common for 'ownerless' infrastructure to be appropriated

Two mixed trends were visible during this period. In large cities, the funeral market continued its development and enlargement. The market for funeral services had its lobbyists; professional associations appeared and infrastructure was developing. At the same time, in small cities, competition and the simplification of production and services significantly increased. In some of these regions, there was effective cessation of all legislation on funerals.

4.1.3 2014 onward

The starting point of this period is 2014 – the annexation of Crimea by Russia and subsequent economic sanctions imposed by Western countries. Since that time, the importation of various funeral accessories to Russia has reduced substantially. Between 2013 and 2020, the Russian ruble was devalued against the U.S. dollar, degrading household purchasing capacity. This economic context was reflected in the funeral industry.

It is also worth recognizing that the period from 2014 to the present day is characterized by a particular internal policy of the government and the presidency of Vladimir Putin. The state is actively nationalizing various assets. There is a high level of corruption, and many officials share business interests with representatives of the police and the Federal Security Bureau. The funeral business is no exception. Many large companies went bankrupt in the 2000s: for example, the companies VMK (public-private) and Gorbrus (private). Some companies entered into private/state ownership, continuing the development of monopoly providers in the larger cities, while stagnation continued in small cities and rural areas.

We can claim that there are three segments of the funeral market:

1 Large private/state companies;
2 Smaller 'legitimate' businesses operating within a clearly well-developed market; and
3 An organized criminal element.

It is essential to take the context into account when attempting to cover different actors of the funeral industry and their primary functions.

4.2 Professional associations

In Russia, there are several professional funeral associations. These associations are divided by geographical features (for example, North-West Russia) or by the type of the service (for instance, manufacturers of accessories).

The biggest of these is the non-profit organization the Union of Funeral Organizations and Crematoria (*Союз крематориев и похоронных организаций*). The Union began operations in 2003, and since that time nearly 300 companies from all parts of Russia have become members. The Union provides advisory and legal assistance to business entities and local governments, business planning, design of funeral homes, vocational training, and the organization of regional seminars. In 2012, the Union of Funeral Organizations and Crematoria became a member of the FIAT-IFTA International Federation of Thanatological Associations.

The Union has lobbied for better standards of service delivery but has had limited success. In 2014, the Union developed a bill proposing the return of a few things (licensing, vocational education and professional standards, and permit to open private cemeteries), but this was not accepted. The Association publishes several professional magazines including *Requiem*, *Funeral Home*, and *Pantheon*. There is an online 'Funeral portal', which is a news portal about the funeral services market.[1]

4.3 Exhibitions and professional events

A national funeral exhibition – 'Necropol' (Necropolis) – operates as a franchise and is held in several cities throughout the year. It is a reasonably large exhibition and is staged over a few days. The exhibition represents mainly manufacturers of coffins, monuments, as well as stonemasons and funeral hearses and is aimed at smaller funeral directors. Within the framework of the exhibition, various contests (for example, among make-up artists) and mourning fashion shows are held. Such exhibitions were popular in the 2000s. Since the mid-2010s the attendance of this kind of exhibition, as well as the number of display stands, has been declining. The exhibition in Moscow is visited by about 12,000 people annually.

4.4 Education

Being a funeral director in modern Russia is not a profession: a special education is not needed. Some colleges and private educational centers provide the opportunity to obtain a funeral director diploma. Tuition in such courses lasts from three to six months. Chiefly, the courses cover the underlying legislation in the field of funeral and funeral culture in different religions and psychology. For example, a funeral services training center operates in Novosibirsk. It is a private center under one of the first private crematoria in Russia. This center issues a diploma of additional education. Courses cost 35,000–50,000 ₽ (the equivalent of $500–800) and take 30–40 academic hours.

4.5 Manufacturers: gravestones and monuments

There are a few large monument manufacturers in Russia: the biggest company is the Danila Master stone company, producing around 25,000 monuments a year. But such big manufacturers are not commonplace. More often, monument installation companies are small businesses engaging 2–4 people, where profits are shared.

Manufacturing of the gravestones and monuments is the least profitable business in the Russian funeral industry.[2] The seasonal earnings amount to an average of 1.5–2.5m ₽ ($20,000-$25,000) for the period. Business is seasonal

Figure 4.1 Gravestone workshop.

Source: Photo from the author's own collection.

and lasts from April to September. An essential part of the business is the setting up of iron fences, which are very common in Russian cemeteries. Stone for monuments is purchased in Karelia and the Caucasus or imported from China. As a rule, such shops and manufacturers are located near the cemeteries. They generally have an agreement with the administration of the cemetery allowing for installation of monuments; in the vast majority of cases, it would be difficult to erect a monument independently of these agreements. The exception is the elite large memorial complexes. The average cost of a gravestone with installation is about 70,000–110,000 ₽ ($1000–1500).

4.6 Manufacturers: coffin producers and accessories

The manufacture of coffins and other accessories includes some large official manufacturers (for example, LiMoKo), but a great deal of production is very local. In most cases, these are reasonably small manufacturing businesses, carried out in the shadow sector of the economy. Some big funeral providers prefer to make the coffins they use. The first state standard on the production of coffins was adopted only in 2019 (GOST R 58392–2019). However, official certification and following the state standard are optional.

Figure 4.2 Coffin Production Small Private Workshop.
Source: Photo from the author's own collection.

4.7 Private funeral directors

There is no state registration of funeral companies in Russia, and limited statistics are available on the scale of the industry. No one knows how many companies and how many people work in this area.

There are different types of non-government funeral arrangements:

- Individual directors. There are individuals who have a shop-front, work with family members, and maintain staff 'in house' to supply those services. They do not have their own infrastructure other than a van which is used as a hearse. They hold 3–4 funerals a month. Such funeral director generally work in small towns and villages (1,000–5,000 population).
- Small funeral homes where an individual with an expanded network will coordinate the supply of driving, coffin supply, and gravedigging as needed from individual contractors on an ad hoc basis and informally. This agency employs several hired people. There is a car, and maybe small-scale handicraft production of coffins and monuments. There may be a private small shop near the cemetery. Such agencies are common in cities from 5,000–50,000 population.
- Big funeral homes and funeral coops. Such funeral organizations have two or more funeral teams (driver, manager), up to several dozen. Such large companies have their own infrastructure (production, storage, farewell hall, and so on). They work in cities with a population of 200,000 people.
- The shadow funeral market in Russia is represented by 'black agents'.[3] These are 'independent funeral directors', without legal status, who organize the funeral individually. They buy information about the death of a person from the police, in morgues, in ambulances, or have a permanent informant. Black agents form working networks: they know where to rent a hearse, quickly buy a coffin, and how to organize a burial in a cemetery. They communicate with each other in chats on Whatsapp, Telegram, etc. The number of such agents amounts to tens of thousands. Their main difference from funeral agencies is the free exchange of resources. They do not have their material base or infrastructure so they use someone else's infrastructure on a rental basis. Large companies are always fighting against them, but this struggle is unsuccessful. Despite the bad image that monopolies create for black agents, they continue to exist and receive orders.[4] Competition is very high in Russia. There arefive to six funeral 'independent funeral directors' for one deceased.

Figure 4.3 Small funeral agency, Kaluga, Central Russia.

Source: Photo from the author's own collection.

Figure 4.4 Funeral agency in the territory of a rural cemetery. The office is located in the trailer, Kaluga, Central Russia.

Source: Photo from the author's own collection.

The owner's income level is comparable to small businesses: cafes, restaurants, repair shops. In a month, the owner of a regional funeral agency receives from 150,000 ₽ to 250,000 ₽. The average salary in the observed region is 35,000 ₽.

The salary of technical personnel (members of the funeral team) is 35,000 ₽ to 70,000 ₽. Funeral agencies constitute a low-profit business. The average cost of a funeral is about 70,000 ₽. The number of funerals is 30–40 per month. The bulk of the income goes to maintaining informal ties at all infrastructure facilities, which costs about 20,000 ₽ to 40,000 ₽ for each funeral (for police, in mortuary, and so on).

4.8 Criminality

The funeral industry in Russia is notorious as one of the most criminalized markets. In many ways, this opinion is a legacy of the 1990s and rampant street crime and stereotypes. However, it would be entirely wrong to deny the enormous influence of organized crime on the funeral industry.

The funeral industry is attractive to criminality because of weak legislative regulations, a large load of ownerless infrastructure, and the ability to evade taxes. In the 1990s, many of the small criminal gangs founded small firms in Russian cities. Many of these companies still exist. For example, a Moscow businessman and one of the founders of the first private crematorium in Russia, Yuri Manilov, was repeatedly accused of extortion. The Moscow funeral company 'Ritual Service' in the 1990s was created by Olga Schneider, the wife of Semyon Mogilevich, one of the leaders of all post-Soviet Mafiosi. 'Ritual Service' is now jointly owned by the state and Oleg Shelyagov, who can be seen in photographs with the leaders of the Solntsevo criminal gang. Another example is the Yekaterinburg company 'Ritual', founded by Viktor Bublik, a former lawyer in companies associated with the criminal group UralMash.[5]

Over the past 30 years, many post-Soviet gangs have gone from street groups to legitimate companies. Many mafiosi gained seats in government bodies. Their funeral companies also became prominent market participants.

4.9 Local governments and municipalities funeral services

The participation of the state (municipalities) in organizing funerals is expressed in two practices:

*   Different municipal utilities that provide free funeral services and maintain the infrastructure of cemeteries. There are such services in

almost all municipalities. As a rule, they are incapable of meeting their responsibilities due to poor funding.

• State employees use their formal role within the funeral infrastructure to develop their own agency business on the side; or even more informally an individual may simply arrange a funeral if they see a short-term business opportunity arising from, for example simply knowing about a death and being in a position to be able to draw together all the required elements.

Government officials are also important informal players in the funeral arrangements, providing services formally and also in some instances informally selling services and preferential treatment for additional fees. These are representatives of local governments and employees of morgues, cemeteries, local bureaucratic apparatuses, and police. The following points show how they take part in the funeral process and how they benefit from it.

Body transportation. The police and doctors record the fact of death and are the first to come to the place of death if it is not a hospital. Information is sold to funeral agents.

State mortuary. Mortuary employees are required to provide body preservation services. Therefore, they often require payment for the body to be released in a timely fashion. As a rule, funeral agents have informal contacts in morgues, and part of the money to pay for such services is included in the cost of the funeral. In some cases, morgue pathologists themselves open a funeral home, selling coffins, various accessories in the morgue, and promoting funeral make-up.

Municipality. Informal participation of government representatives often occurs during the registration of the burial in the cemetery (registration of a place in a cemetery takes place in municipal services). Cemetery plots are free of charge, but a municipality official can request payment help to identify the best place among all the free ones.

4.10 Cemetery workers

There are no private cemeteries in Russia. Municipalities maintain cemeteries. Local authorities create special services for the administration of cemeteries. These services distribute places and dig graves. In Russia, most commonly, the grave is dug and backfilled manually. Cemetery workers also sell grave maintenance services and the installation and repairing of fences and monuments.

There is no law that would prohibit an outsider from digging a grave. However, it is the municipal cemetery workers who usually dig the grave.

They are often involved in the underground economy and offer various additional services, such as clearing fallen trees.

4.11 Innovation and digitalization in Russian funeral industry

4.11.1 Digitalization

Large players in the funeral market are starting to offer services through websites and provide clients with online shopping and ordering services. For example, a large company in the Moscow market (Ritual.ru) has in recent years introduced extensive advertising on the internet. Ritual.ru is also trying to develop the B2B (business to business) sector by offering various funeral accessories for agents through its mobile app. Another example is 'Honest Agent', a company that has developed a mobile application for agents, facilitating speedy ordering of coffins, funeral transport, and grave spaces. These developments are digitizing existing informal cooperative ties among independent funeral agents themselves.

4.11.2 New services

New developments, including green burial, eco-funerals, or ashes disposal, are rare in the Russian funeral industry. There appears to be limited demand

Figure 4.5 Spaceway company.
Source: Photo from the author's own collection.

for eco-funerals, and the regulatory framework does not encourage the development of new types of burial spaces. Ashes, according to federal law, can only be buried in the ground, stored in a columbarium, or scattered. However, the Spaceway company, a new venture, sells ashes dispersal in the stratosphere via a launch up to the height of 30 kilometers.

In 2015, Russian designer and web developer Iskander Kadyrov opened the Voyager company. It produces exclusive futuristic coffins costing from 1,000,000 ₽ ($14,000). Unfortunately, information is not available on the number of models sold.[6]

Cryonics services are also being promoted in Russia. Since 2006, the CryoRus company has offered body preservation services in special cryo-freezers. In 2020, 72 people became clients of CryoRus.[7] Ecological funerals, alkaline hydrolysis, and other types of disposal of dead bodies are not common and are not regulated by law.

Some entrepreneurs are trying to scale the funeral business and offer franchises. It is a package proposal, which includes ready-made operational solutions, branding, and typical agency construction. The founder of the Cranes Agency, Ilya Boltunov, is attempting to develop a franchise model, with limited success (https://guravli.com/).

4.12 Consumer assessment of the quality of services in the funeral market

Marketing research of the funeral market in Russia is not developed. However, in 2015 and by order of the mayor's office, a public opinion poll was conducted in Moscow. This poll attempted to estimate the level of consumer satisfaction and understand the view of the public on problems in the funeral market. The poll had 1100 informants.[8] The problems described are in evidence across the whole of Russia. The survey indicated that the main problems were:

* Abandoned cemeteries;
* lack of burial places;
* corruption;
* small amount of social payment for a funeral;
* problems transporting the body from the morgue to the cemetery (long distances); and
* bureaucracy.

In general, the authority of the funeral directors is rather low. Consumers are very distrustful of funeral directors and funeral agents. Buyers expect fraud, inflated prices, and a lack of transparency, and arranging a funeral is regarded as being highly stressful. In this regard, there is pressure on the state to offer a better level of protection to consumers and regulation of providers

Notes

1 https://funeralportal.ru/ acc. 25 May 2021.
2 This statement is based on the author's own observations during field research, as well as on publications in the media. For example. https://cutt.ly/YdS7P67 acc. 25 May 2021.
3 'Black Agent' is a well-established name for illegal funeral directors.
4 In my opinion, black agents are one of the few examples of the free market in Russia: they are united, support each other against monopolies, are able to cooperate against giant competitors and obtain resource exchange networks.
5 'A coffin, a cemetery, hundreds of billions of rubles: How bureaucrats, siloviki and thugs divide the funeral market'. https://novayagazeta.ru/articles/2019/06/08/80819-grob-kladbische-sotni-milliardov-rubley acc. April 6, 2021.
6 'These Russian companies are offering exotic funerals to send you off in style'. www.rbth.com/business/329484-exotic-funerals acc. April 6, 2021.
7 List of people cryopreserved in 'KrioRus'. http://kriorus.ru/Krionirovannye-lyudi acc. 6 April 2021.
8 'The opinion of the inhabitants of Moscow about the funeral industry in the city'. www.mos.ru/upload/documents/files/1676/ritual.pdf acc. April 6, 2021.

5 Cemeteries

We should not underestimate the influence of the Soviet heritage on contemporary Russia. The Russian Federation inherited dozens of institutional problems of the USSR. One of the most pivotal problems for our field is the problem of ownerless infrastructure. Rapid Soviet industrialization developed thousands of infrastructural objects. The major part of infrastructural objects in the USSR was constructed and built up by different factories and large production clusters that were responsible for them. A significant share of the infrastructure was built within the collective farms that regulated the process themselves. Such infrastructural objects were not projected under a unified quality standard. After the USSR collapsed, an extensive share of such industrial clusters was closed and infrastructural objects lost their owners: an estimated 50 percent of infrastructure objects – including roads, pipes, and electricity networks – have ownerless status.[1] It means that it is impossible to indicate the owner of these objects or a person/company who is responsible for their work. Olga Molyarenko also noted that such a situation is a consequence of the failure of several municipality reforms in Russia.[2]

The infrastructural problem of ownerless objects is a central issue for funeral arrangements in contemporary Russia too. At the moment of the USSR collapse, municipalities in new Russia had inherited thousands of illegal cemeteries, access roads to cemeteries, and so on. For municipalities, it means that they have to legalize them and find the money for their maintenance. For different reasons, municipalities are reluctant to do it. I will now attempt to describe general observations of how such objects are looking and functioning in contemporary Russia.

5.1 Burial sites types

Burial sites types

- Churchyards
    - Pre-October Revolution churchyards

DOI: 10.4324/9781003153672-5

- Disaster

  - Epidemic
  - Battlefield

- Denominational/minority ethnic (as a rule, these are separate areas within large necropolises)

  - Christian
  - Jewish
  - Muslim
  - Pagan or local ethnic cemeteries

- Institutional

  - Monastic
  - Hospital
  - Military barracks
  - Prison cemeteries

- Cemeteries

  - Municipal
  - Ownerless
  - National necropolises

- War cemeteries

  - Russian
  - German
  - Alien

- Columbariums

5.2 Number of burial sites

It is generally unknown how many cemeteries are in the Russian Federation. It is also unclear which of these cemeteries are open and which are closed for burial. There are various estimates: the Ministry of Construction claims that there are only 72,000 cemeteries in Russia, and the Union of Funeral Organizations and Crematoriums[3] speaks of 600,000 different burial places. Their total area constitutes about 1m hectares. About 35,000 people work in cemeteries including the shadow economy.[4]

5.3 Ownership and management

The majority of cemeteries in Russia today do not have an owner. They are not registered in municipal ownership, and maps rarely show that cemeteries exist. Ownerless cemeteries entail problems for everyone. Local authorities are unable to allocate funding to cemetery maintenance if ownership is uncertain. For residents, there are problems with burial. In the jurisprudence of the Russian Federation, there are hundreds of court cases relating to parties trying to establish the status of burial sites.[5]

Cemeteries are also a subject of economic dispute for various government departments that are trying to discharge them from the books. Further, Russian law guarantees every citizen a free burial place, which means that cemeteries practically do not generate income in the legal market. In addition to this, there are no regulations defining a responsibility for ongoing maintenance; cemeteries can simply appear, with no legal framework (Figure 4.1). Illegal cemeteries exist in every region. The lack of architectural planning during the construction of these cemeteries means that they are often flooded, there is no ongoing maintenance, the site contains no internal pathways or roadways, and there may not be a formal access road to the site.[6]

Control of ownerless cemeteries often falls to criminal groups, which sell burial plots, distribute burial places, and try to keep the cemetery in good condition. Users of the cemetery do not necessarily notice who controls the cemetery exactly.

5.4 The grave

The 'Recommendations on the order of burial and the maintenance of cemeteries in the Russian Federation' (GosStroy Russia, MDK 11–01.2002) regulate the standards for the depth, width, and height of the grave:

- The depth of the grave should not exceed 2.2 meters, and the distance to groundwater is at least 0.5 meters. The minimum depth is 1.5 meters;
- The height of the embankment designed to protect against surface water should not exceed 0.5 meters;
- The width of the grave should be at least 1 meter;
- In length, its dimensions should be at least 2 meters;
- Usually the grave is located so that the head of the deceased is to the west, and the legs to the east. This is a Christian tradition. A monument (cross) can stand both at the feet and at the head.

However, it is crucial to emphasize that these recommendations are often not complied with. The depth of the grave is often from 1 meter to 2 meters deep, depending on the season. Much depends on the neighboring sites: in old cemeteries there may be little space for a new burial. In this case, the undertakers move monuments and fences to make room.

5.5 Layout

5.5.1 Churchyards

Very few churchyards have survived in Russia. Burials are not carried out on them, and the Soviet government destroyed most of the gravestones as well as churches. The surviving churchyards are architectural monuments and may contain memorial sculptures, crypts, and marble crosses. The size of the graveyards is no more than 3–4 hectares. There is no general burial register, but church books include the names of those buried in the churchyard.

5.5.2 Cemeteries

Within this ownership context, the appearance of cemeteries varies substantially. The size of cemeteries varies from half a hectare to 350 hectares (the Northern cemetery in Rostov-on-Don). The most common cemetery size is 30 hectares. The cemeteries outside the city are much larger than the cemeteries in the city.

As a rule, Russian cemeteries have one central entrance; they are fenced with a metal fence or wall (if they are not in the field or in the forest). At the entrance to the cemetery there is a parking lot, an administration building, and several shops that sell tombstones and monuments. A small church may also be located on the site, but in general there are no places for a farewell ceremony in cemeteries.

Cemeteries have several main zones. In the center is the tomb of the unknown soldier and a monument to the victims of World War II. Large cemeteries include several military burial sites. The central part also contains the graves of honored citizens. Some cemeteries make sites for children's graves. Gypsies and Armenians often have their own separate plots. The graves of unidentified people are in a separate section of the cemetery.

Russian cemeteries have several walking paths. But most of the graves are randomly located and access to them is not always easy. Usually, cemetery administration and visitors do not plant trees or shrubs, and there is no decorative landscaping. However, families often plant fresh flowers on the graves.

5.5.3 Denominational and religious cemeteries

The law permits the creation of a confessional cemetery, and many religious communities take this opportunity. In large cities, there are not only separate religious sites in municipal cemeteries but also separate cemeteries: for

Figure 5.1 A funeral in a cemetery located in a field.
Source: Photo from the author's own collection.

example, Muslim and Jewish. Separate cemeteries are established and operated by the municipality at the request of the local community.

5.5.4 Military cemeteries and national necropolises

The Federal Military Memorial Cemetery in Borisovka, Moscow Region, is a modern national necropolis. This cemetery was created in 2013. It is the largest military cemetery in Russia, intended for the burial of retired and active high-ranking employees of the Armed Forces of Russia, the USSR, and citizens who have undertaken especially essential state services to the country.

This cemetery has a good layout: there are plots for different branches of the army, and wide walking alleys are provided. The main cemetery memorial is the Bridge of Heroes. It depicts warriors of different historical periods. The area of the cemetery is 55 hectares and has the capacity for 40,000 burials. Tombstone design follows a recommended pattern with the use of bas-relief or bust. This cemetery is closed to the public.

Figure 5.2 Typical burial plot.
Source: Photo from the author's own collection.

Among the historical cemeteries of Russia, six memorial necropolises with military graves can be highlighted. They are located in Moscow (two of them), St. Petersburg, Volgograd, Sevastopol, Kaliningrad.

Notable war cemeteries include:

- *Federal War Memorial Cemetery of the Ministry of Defense of the Russian Federation, Moscow.* It is a single pantheon complex, created according to a carefully designed project, and accepts new burials in accordance with regulatory documents.
- *Piskaryovskoye Memorial Cemetery, St Petersburg.* This large-scale necropolis has the mass graves of World War II victims of the Siege of Leningrad and soldiers of the Leningrad Front.
- *The Sestroretsk Military Memorial Cemetery, St Petersburg.* This contains Russian military graves, a sculptural monument, and a bunker of the Great Patriotic War.
- *Memorial Cemetery at Mamayev Kurgan, Volgograd.* This necropolis is a mass burial of 1,500 Soviet soldiers who died during the defense of Stalingrad. Here, with due honors, burials of the remains found by

search groups are also made. This site contains 'The Motherland Calls' statue, erected in 1967 and at that time the largest free-formed sculpture in the world.

- *Sevastopol Memorial Cemetery.* Contains the mass graves of participants in the defense and liberation of the city during the Crimean War. The site also has places for the burial of veterans of the Great Patriotic War.
- *The Memorial Cemetery 'Barrow of Glory', Kaliningrad.* This site has a large mass grave that accommodates reburial of the remains of Soviet soldiers found by search units in the Kaliningrad region.

A vast number of military cemeteries appeared following World War II. Many of these cemeteries included special cities for mass graves of unknown soldiers. In Russia, such burials have a special state status. There is a World War II monument in every village; most of these monuments are homemade.

5.5.5 Disused cemeteries

There are many cemeteries closed for burial in Russia, and these are often located within cities. These sites are closed because they have no more space but it is still possible to bury an urn with ashes or a coffin in a relative's grave. For example, almost all cemeteries within the borders of Moscow are closed to new burials but continued burial can take place in family graves.

There are no completely closed and disused cemeteries where burials cannot be made at all. An exception may be cemeteries in abandoned cities and villages, although, in law, these sites are still open for the burial of cremated ashes or in a family grave.

5.5.6 Reused burial plots

Reuse of the grave is provided for by federal law. For this, at least 20 years must pass, and the grave must be declared ownerless. The status of an ownerless burial is assigned if there is no care for the grave for ten years (there may be regional differences). The problem of abandoned graves is quite serious. According to estimates for 2015, the total area of abandoned graves is about 25,000 hectares.[7]

Notes

1 O. A. Molyarenko (2017) 'Ownerless highways in Russia', *ECO*, 4:514, 88–109. (Моляренко О. А. Бесхозяйные автомобильные дороги в России // ЭКО. 2017. № 4 (514). С. 88–109).

2 O. A. Molyarenko (2017) 'State practices of constructing statistical illusions, or "dead zones" of domestic statistics', *Sociological Journal*, 23:4, 104–120. (Моляренко О. А. Государственные практики конструирования статистических иллюзий, или «мёртвые зоны» отечественной статистики // Социологический журнал. 2017. Т. 23. № 4. С. 104–120).

3 'This is a professional association of workers in the funeral industry, which was quite influential in the 2000s'. http://pohoronotrasl-souz.ru/ acc. April 6, 2021.

4 G. N. Syutkin (2016) *Funeral Business Fundamentals*. Tutorial, Moscow: Infra-M, Alpha-M, 320. (Сюткин Г.Н. Основы ритуально-похоронного дела. Учебное пособие. – Москва:Инфра-М, Альфа-М, 2016.- 320с).

5 S. V. Mokhov and V. Zotova (2017) 'The case of the fence, table and bench: Modes of justice in the practice of allocating places in a cemetery', *Journal of Social Policy Research*, 15:1, 21–36. (Мохов С. В., Зотова В. Дело об ограде, столике и скамье: режимы справедливости в практиках распределения мест на кладбище // Журнал исследований социальной политики. 2017. Т. 15. No 1. С. 21−36).

6 Public Television of Russia (2016) 'In the Rostov region, the farmer will sue the funeral home, which established a cemetery in his field' [В Ростовской области фермер будет судиться с похоронной конторой, которая устроила кладбище на его поле]. https://otr-online.ru/news/v-rostovskoi-oblasti-ppart-72360.html acc. April 6, 2021.

7 'Ministry of Construction proposes to seize and cremate remains from abandoned graves' [Минстрой предлагает изымать и кремировать останки из заброшенных могил]. https://iz.ru/news/584670.

6 Crematoriums

As mentioned in the historical chapter, the cremation movement is not developed in Russia. Over the past 30 years after the collapse of the USSR, several dozen crematoria have been opened. However, this process is very slow. It is difficult to open a new crematorium due to serious opposition from the Orthodox Church and because of the lack of transparent legislation for opening a private crematorium.

6.1 Ownership and management

There are currently 27 crematoria in Russia in 23 cities. Three of them are private (Novosibirsk, Tula, Moscow), and nine of them are under a public-private partnership. The rest of the crematoria are run by the state (municipalities). Twelve crematoria have opened over the past ten years (see Table 6.1).

There was a private mobile crematorium in Kaliningrad. A local funeral agency uses a vehicle with a cremator installed in it, offering a cremation procedure for 15,000 ₽ ($200). For several years, this crematorium operated illegally until it was finally banned by local authorities.

For the most part, cremation services are not popular: on average, relatives choose to cremate in no more than 15–20 percent of cases. The most significant percentage is observed in St. Petersburg, Norilsk, and Moscow (50–70 percent of all deaths).[1] The main criterion for choosing cremation or burial is the cost of the service. Cremation, like everywhere else in the world, is cheaper. The cost of cremation in Moscow ranges from 14,000 ₽ to 40,000 ₽ ($200 to $400), depending on the lease of the farewell hall.[2]

6.2 Crematorium layout

Most crematoria inherited the traditional Soviet architecture: constructivism. As a rule, these are concrete buildings with no windows. Little attention

DOI: 10.4324/9781003153672-6

Table 6.1 Crematoria currently operating in Russia with year of opening and ownership

Moscow suburbs (Nikolo-Arkhangelsky)	1972	State
St Petersburg	1973	State
Yekaterinburg	1982	State
Moscow (Mitinsky)	1985	State
Moscow (Khovansky)	1988	State
Nizhny Tagil	1988	State
Moscow suburbs (Nosovikhinsky)	1998	Private
Rostov-on-Don	2000	State
Vladivostok (Artyom)	2001	State
Novokuznetsk	2002	State
Vladivostok	2002	State
Norilsk	2002	State
Novorossiysk	2003	State
Novosibirsk (Novosibirsk)	2003	Public-private partnership
Chelyabinsk	2007	Public-private partnership
Surgut	2008	State
Volgograd	2011	Public-private partnership
Tula	2013	Private
Khabarovsk	2014	State
Novosibirsk (Zakamensky)	2015	State
Yaroslavl	2015	Public-private partnership
Arkhangelsk	2015	State
Barnaul	2015	Public-private partnership
Nizhny Novgorod	2017	Public-private partnership
Magnitogorsk	2017	Public-private partnership
Simferopol	2018	Public-private partnership
Voronezh	2020	Public-private partnership

has been paid to the design and appearance of the crematorium, and it is customary to use a lot of stone and marble.

Most crematoria are small and have one farewell room. This is a large hall with a pedestal for the coffin in the center. There are chairs. Crematoria usually perform 40–60 cremations per month and use Czech Tabo-SC ovens running on gas.

The largest crematorium – Nikolo-Arkhangelsky – is equipped with seven double cremation ovens. Its construction was completed in March 1972. This crematorium performs about 70 cremations per day. This is the largest crematorium in Russia and Europe. The crematorium has a toilet, waiting rooms, an administration building, body preparation rooms, a funeral accessories store, and ten farewell halls. There is a place for an orchestra, with chairs and a table.

6.3 Crematorium service

The crematoria are open from 9am to 7pm. Average waiting time is about 1.5 hours (despite the schedule and booking time, there are always time shifts). The farewell lasts about 15–20 minutes. The priest is usually not invited to serve in the crematorium, but there is such an opportunity. Farewell is conducted by a special employee of the crematorium. He reads parting words and gives the family time to say goodbye to the deceased person.

It is possible to order music. In the larger Moscow crematoria, this is an orchestra: the choice of music consists of 10–12 famous lyric pieces of music. Small crematoria use CD players.

6.4 Disposal of ashes

The usual ways of disposing of ashes are keeping the urn at home, storing the urn in a columbarium, or burying it in the ground. Columbaria are rare and only available in cities which have crematoria. For example, in Moscow, where there are five crematoria, about 29 out of 136 cemeteries have columbaria. There are no legal private columbaria, but some funeral agencies also offer the service of storing urns.

Columbariums are a wall with urn niches. Niches are usually covered with black granite plaques resembling small gravestones. A niche is rented indefinitely. The cost of the service is from 20,000 ₽ to 100,000 ₽ ($250 to $1500) at once, plus annually 700 ₽ ($90) are paid to this amount.

Notes

1 Unfortunately, there are no official statistics.
2 'Cremation is cheaper than burial'. www.kommersant.ru/doc/1952216 acc. April 6, 2021.

7 Transportation, mortuaries, and farewell halls

7.1 Transporting coffins and bodies

Transportation of a dead body (whether from the place of death to the morgue or from the morgue to the cemetery or crematorium) is an essential element of the funeral infrastructure in contemporary Russia. As a rule, transporting a dead body from the place of death to the morgue is a paid service. The Federal Law does not provide free services for the removal of bodies of the deceased to the morgue for a forensic examination or autopsy. Therefore, charging for this service is legal and presents a specific business opportunity. Ready availability with transport is essential for securing funeral business since it is generally the case that the first individual to respond to a death receives the order for the funeral. It is notable that the purchase/sale of information about death is widespread in Russia, and this is the primary source of receiving orders; indeed, information is often sold more than once. Transport is essential, since there are often vast distances between main infrastructure facilities: there may be 50 kilometers between the road and the cemetery, for example.

Despite the fact that the production of funeral hearses has not been established in the USSR, an alternative industry has developed in the modification of vehicles to facilitate the transportation of bodies. In Soviet times, freight transport – from small trucks and buses to tractors – was used for this purpose. In contemporary Russia, it is more common to use small minibuses converted for transportation of the coffin: funeral companies re-equip the bus interior in order to fit the coffin.

Regulations are in place to ensure sanitary operation of funeral transport, but compliance levels are low. For example, all hearse buses must have a bactericidal lamp and undergo regular sanitization, and should not be used for anything other than transporting a dead body. However, specially converted vehicles tend to exist in large cities only; in rural areas old Soviet practices continue.

DOI: 10.4324/9781003153672-7

Figure 7.1 Special vehicle for transporting a dead body to the morgue.

Source: Photo from the author's own collection.

Figure 7.2 Author of this book with Ilya Boltunov, a funeral director from Kaluga.
          A hearse made from a van can be seen in the background.

Source: Photo from the author's own collection.

The conversion of buses and minibuses for use as hearses is provided by several companies in Russia: for example, InvestAvto. The cost of a Russian GAZ car converted for a hearse is about 1 million ₽, or about $13,000. Box 7.1 lists the elements included in a standard hearse conversion.[1]

Box 7.1 Elements included in a standard hearse conversion

• Colour scheme	• Six seats	• Handrail at entrance
• Circular glazing of car body	• Podium with handrail and drawer for coffin	• Applying faux leather to interior
• Tinted windows	• Bacterial lamp, 220v	• Voltage converter, 220v
• Addition of side step	• Ventilation hatch	• Interior lights
• 'Autoline' floor covering	• Antifreeze heater from the engine cooling system.	

The hearse is also used for transportation from the place of death to the morgue on the day of the funeral. Hearse rental costs from 1,000 ₽ to 4,000 ₽ per hour depending on the region and brand of car.

7.2 Morgues and places to store dead bodies

There are three types of storage facilities for dead bodies.

- Mortuaries are located in either hospitals or forensic facilities. Morgues that exist in hospitals might also include facilities for forensic examination and are usually in a separate building on hospital sites. There are forensic morgues to establish the causes of death where there is a suspicion of crime entailed. These morgues are likely to have several technical rooms for staff and large rooms for storing bodies.
- There are commercial and state funeral services with facilities that include body storage, often of very poor quality. Many funeral companies store dead bodies in cars with refrigerators. This type of organization also provides commercial services for preparing the body for a funeral, which will be considered in Chapter 9.
- There are people operating much less formally who simply sell space they have modified to facilitate body storage. This final provision is evidently illegal, but still common. For example, in the city of Suvorov, a local entrepreneur has equipped a private morgue in her garage and

Figure 7.3 State morgue. The room where dead bodies are stored.

Source: Photo from the author's own collection.

Figure 7.4 State morgue. The room where dead bodies are stored.

Source: Photo from the author's own collection.

periodically pays a fine of 5,000 ₽.[2] Another man in Nizhny Novgorod has also equipped storage for corpses in a garage.

7.3 Farewell halls

The funeral hall is a particular room for holding a ceremony of farewell or requiem to the deceased. Mourning halls are located in many medical and funeral institutions. Premises at morgues and hospitals usually may house a ceremony for 20–30 people, while the mourning halls at Moscow crematoria and the central clinical hospital can accommodate hundreds of participants. For the convenience of those who pay their last respects, the mourning hall is often connected with auxiliary rooms: a freezer, a room for preparing the body, and sometimes also a restroom. Usually, mourning halls have a modest character including a coffin pedestal, speakers (if the orchestra is not used), and chairs for participants.

Funeral agencies sometimes operate their own small farewell halls. The regulations indicate that such rooms should be located 50 meters away from residential dwellings and must undergo sanitization in advance. However, many funeral agencies infringe on these rules and open farewell halls in their offices, irrespective of location.

Where a funeral is taking place of a noted individual, it is also common for use to be made of a venue suggested by the professional activities of the deceased: for example, it is customary to pay last respects to a deceased artist in a theater, to a movie actor in the Cinema House, to a famous writer in the Central House of Artists, to an athlete in the sports arena, clubhouse, etc.

Notes

1 'Complete sets and photos can be found on the website of one of the manufacturers'. https://luidorbus.ru/product/ritualnyy-transport/ritualnyy-avtobus-gazel-next/ acc. April 6, 2021.
2 S. Mokhov (2021) *Archeology of Russian Death: Ethnography of the Funeral Industry in Contemporary Russia.* Moscow: Common Place (Мохов С. *Археология русской смерти. Этнография похоронного дела в современной России.* Москва: Common place, 2021).

8 Religious belief and funerary practices

8.1 Russian Orthodox Church

The overwhelming majority of Russian citizens are Orthodox. About 66 percent of the population defines itself as Orthorox.[1] The Russian Orthodox Church (ROC) has about 310 dioceses, about 38,000 parishes (in the ROC, one parish means one temple or church), and almost a thousand monasteries. The diocesan boundaries are almost coterminous with the regional map of the Russian Federation. The main difference lies in the fact that the European part of Russia is divided into a larger number of dioceses than the number of regions.

The Russian Orthodox Church is developing very rapidly in contemporary Russia. Researchers calculated that ROC opens three new churches per day and almost 1,000 new parishes a year. The actual growth in 30 years after the collapse of the USSR is 2,300 percent. The construction of new churches in the living areas of large cities often leads to conflicts with local residents since the ROC is actively building churches in Muslim regions too, including Tatarstan and Bashkiria. The exception is the North Caucasus (Chechnya, Dagestan), where 99 percent of the population is Muslim. The Russian Orthodox Church has no data on the number of its members or attendance at services.

However, despite its active development, the ROC does not seek to return cemeteries under its control or to participate formally in the funeral business. News stories report local priests being involved in the funeral business, and selling coffins, funeral clothes, and crosses right on the territory of the church. In this regard, they are similar to workers in morgues and municipalities.[2]

8.2 Christian farewell

Priests actively participate in farewell. In most cases, the farewell takes place not in the church but in the cemetery: the priest is invited directly to

DOI: 10.4324/9781003153672-8

the burial. The Church offers a special Orthodox rite (requiem) called the *otpevanie*, which consists of sequential reading of a series of sacred texts.

This rite is prescribed on the third day after death before burial in a cemetery or crematorium. To conduct an otpevanie, arrangements need to be made in advance with the priest of the chosen church or the parish or at the cemetery. An otpevanie can be ordered in the church itself if the family can supply a medical death certificate or official death certificate.

To conduct an otpevanie, the following is required:

- pectoral cross;
- icon;
- permissive prayer sheet;
- funeral bedspread;
- a piece of paper with a prayer that is put on the forehead; and
- candles.

All of these objects (except candles) are placed in a coffin when carrying the body to the church. Almost all churches offer this opportunity. Sometimes there are small churches in the cemetery, crematorium, or morgue where the priest can perform the ceremony. The otpevanie is optional, but it is essential to mention the church as a key infrastructure point.

It is crucial to emphasize that relatives or friends do not deliver speeches at the farewell in the Orthodox Church – otpevanie is an exclusively religious rite conducted by priests with family participation limited to attendance only.

8.3 Muslim funerals

Islam is the native religion for many residents of the Russian Federation, especially the North Caucasus, Tatarstan, and Bashkiria. About 14 million citizens of the Russian Federation (around 10 percent of population) consider themselves to be Muslims.

Muslims have their own plot areas in cemeteries, as well as completely their own cemeteries. In many Muslim regions, funerals are organized by the local community, so the funeral business is very poorly developed there. The community itself prepares the body, digs a grave, buys a funeral shroud, arranges transportation and farewell. The Muslim grave is prepared in a specific way: a niche is dug to one side at the bottom of the grave so that the earth does not rest on the body. The body is turned to the right and aligned with the feet facing Makkah. This is in contrast to the ROC, which does not participate in the funeral organization.

Contemporary Muslim funeral culture in Russia is heavily influenced by Soviet practices. The monuments are visually similar to civil and Orthodox

Figure 8.1 Farewell (*otpevanie*) takes place in the cemetery near the grave.

Source: Photo from the author's own collection.

gravestones, but with the addition of Islamic symbols – a crescent moon and/ or the shahada or Islamic oath. The main difference in monuments between Orthodox and Muslim is the absence of photographs of the deceased on Muslim monuments. Gravestones companies make, as a rule, separate tombstones for Muslim and for Orthodox.

8.4 Jewish funerals

Jewish funerals are organized by private funeral companies. They adapt the bureaucratic funeral procedures to the requirements of the Jewish tradition. The Jewish community takes over the religious element of the funeral. The burial takes place in separate sections of the cemeteries.

8.5 Pagan funerals

Pagan burials are very rare, but there are still some cases. For example, the Slavic pagan tradition requires the burning of the body on a wood fire. These bonfires are not legal. However, the lack of regulatory bodies in the funeral business leads to the fact that such cases do occur.[3]

Notes

1 'The number of atheists in Russia has doubled in four years'. www.rbc.ru/society/23/03/2021/6059a2fd9a7947c314aab9c4 acc. April 28, 2021.
2 '"I will bury quickly and expensively": Who is fighting with the Russian Orthodox Church for the funeral market?'. https://ria.ru/20170830/1501342182.html acc. April 28, 2021.
3 'In the Kirov region, pagans burned the body of a colleague on a funeral pyre'. www.mk.ru/social/2018/03/05/v-kirovskoy-oblasti-yazychniki-sozhgli-telo-soratnika-na-pogrebalnom-kostre.html.

9 Typical funeral

9.1 Immediately following the death

Russians die at home in about 50–53 percent of cases.[1] Hospitals are ill-equipped and often send seriously ill patients home so as not to spoil the mortality statistics.[2] Dying at home has increased as a consequence of healthcare reform in Russia in 2010–2012, which led to a reduction in the number of beds. Nursing homes are still poorly developed, and there are only 73 hospices in Russia.

If a person dies in a hospital, family members generally are not in attendance at the death. Intensive care units generally remain closed for visits, especially at night. Immediately after death, the body is taken to the morgue. Typically, this is a municipal hospital morgue. The body is transported by a special municipal service or a private funeral director. By law, this is a free service. It is very rare that the body is left at home, but the municipal service may not come to the call for a long time.

9.2 Making funeral arrangements

The contract with the funeral director or agent is signed immediately after death. As a rule, the information about the death is informally reported by the police or medics to the funeral directors or agents. They immediately show up at an apartment or hospital and offer services. The vast majority of people agree with these first suggestions. In Russia, it is not customary to make a choice, compare prices, and bargain for services.

Two essential purchases in preparation for the funeral are a coffin and a wooden cross which is installed on the grave until the monument is built. These two items make up the 'funeral shopping basket'. There is no law on advertising funeral supplies in Russia. Typically, the choice of such things takes place on the spot: customers come and choose a coffin, a cross, and other accessories. The choice is based on the planned amount. That is, if the client, for instance, can afford to spend only 14,000–15,000 ₽ ($200) on

DOI: 10.4324/9781003153672-9

funeral accessories, the funeral director selects a 'funeral set' for him for this sum. In recent years, it has become fashionable to buy a package offer that includes all services, among them a coffin and a cross.

An important part of the preparation is to dig the grave. Cultural and religious characteristics determine the shape and depth of the grave in Russia: as indicated in Chapter 8, the funeral rites of Christians and Muslims differ. There are also differences between grave digging approaches. Sanitary standards also regulate shape and depth. Indubitably, digging a grave is always hard work. Particular hardships arise in winter when frozen ground needs to be warmed up before digging. In Russia, the vast majority of graves are dug by hand. Under the law, cemeteries are managed by the state/municipalities, which set the price for digging the grave. However, this is one of the most corrupted stages of a funeral. The team of diggers often tries to get additional amounts for the elimination of various malfunctions – trees, stones, water from the grave.

Figure 9.1 The author of this book is digging a grave in a winter cemetery.

9.3 Care of the deceased

As a rule, the deceased is shown to the family for a short time only. Until the day of the funeral, the body is in the morgue and is not visited. Preparation of the body for the funeral consists of washing the body, hairdressing, and casketing. The deceased may be shaved and family members bring clothes. Most commonly, these services are performed in the morgue. By law, such services are free, but funeral workers often demand informal fees. In Russia, embalming is not developed as a practice.

9.4 Between the day of death and the funeral

The funeral takes place on the third day after death (if these are not holidays and special services, including the morgue, are working). During these days, family members are busy preparing papers and inviting guests. Invitations are made by phone; postcards and letters are not accepted. Obituaries in papers are also not popular. In recent years, it has become more popular to notify people about a person's death and planned funeral using social media.

Common practices are to cover mirrors with black cloth and to play no music in the house or apartment of the deceased. The photograph of the deceased should be prominently displayed, along with a lit candle, a glass of vodka, black bread, and flowers. Preliminary preparations for the funeral are listed in Box 9.1.

Box 9.1 Preliminary preparations for the funeral

- Transport the body from the place of death, by ambulance or a private funeral company
- Stor the body in a state or private mortuary or in a forensic autopsy morgue (if it is necessary to determine the cause of death)[3]
- Conclude any necessary forensic medical examination
- Secure the medical death certificate
- Appoint a funeral agency (if this has not already happened) and signing a contract
- Secure state death certificate
- Prepare the body including washing, make-up, hairdressing, and clothing, in a funeral home or more often in the mortuary
- If burial is anticipated, (1) inspect the burial place and purchase a plot; (2) complete the necessary paperwork; if cremation is anticipated, choose a crematorium and book a time slot
- Choose a coffin, coffin accessories (handles, bedspread, and so on), cross and hearse
- Invite guests by phone

The average number of guests is 20–30 people who are relatives, friends, and colleagues. As a rule, most of the guests come only to say the last good-bye to the morgue or church (depending on where the farewell takes place). Only family members and close friends come to the cemetery. Anyone can make a cash gift for a family member. However, this is not a common practice.

Figure 9.2 Shop with funeral hardware: crosses, coffins, flowers.
Source: Photo from the author's own collection.

Figure 9.2 (Continued)

9.5 The day of the funeral

The following stages are included on the day of the funeral, depending on whether a burial or cremation is taking place.

Funeral Day (in the case of burial)

- Collecting the deceased from the morgue/obtaining the body from storage;
- Transportation of the deceased to the place of farewell;
- Farewell – in the church/near the house/in the cemetery itself;
- Transfer of the body to the place of burial;
- Farewell near the grave;
- Burial; and
- Funeral dinner

Funeral Day (in the case of cremation)

- Collecting the deceased from the morgue/obtaining the body from storage;
- Transportation of the deceased to the place of farewell;
- Transportation of the deceased to the crematorium;
- Farewell at the crematorium; and
- Funeral dinner

After the funeral

- Memorial dinners on the 9th and 40th day after death;
- Receiving an urn if there has been a cremation and placing it in a columbarium or in the burial ground; and
- Selection, manufacturing, and installation of the monument.

At this point we shall consider some of these stages in more detail.

On the day of the funeral, the body is taken from its 'storage' location back to the family home for a short time if it is possible. In most cases, the funeral begins at the morgue. Guests arrive there in their own cars or public transport. The farewell takes place in the morgue (or in the church). Next, the coffin and the guests travel to the cemetery or crematorium, and then after the service, they go on to a farewell dinner. From the morgue (or from the church), a specially rented bus or van drives guests who do not have private cars. The coffin is carried by the members of the funeral team, friends and colleagues carry the coffin to the grave. Family members do not carry the coffin. Guests wear black. However, there are no strict rules.

The place of farewell (morgue, special hall in the funeral home, temple) is decorated with flowers. Decoration is arranged by the funeral agent. During the farewell, the open coffin stands centrally, and on a special pedestal and the guests approach it in turn. The coffin is open all centrally in the farewell hall. People attending the funeral touch the coffin, kiss the deceased on the forehead, say farewell words. During this time, family members sit on chairs next to the coffin.

The farewell is very typical and standardized and takes about 20–30 minutes at the morgue or church. Guests say short farewell words if desired. Most of the guests are silent. At the grave, the farewell is repeated similarly to the farewell in the morgue or church. The open coffin stands near the grave for about 20 minutes, and everyone approaches the coffin during this time. Sometimes the personal belongings of the deceased, coins, icons are placed in the coffin. Then the lid of the coffin is closed, and it is lowered into the grave on ropes by the funeral team. Each of the guests throws a handful of earth into the grave. The grave is covered with earth by the members of the funeral team (they also lowered the coffin). It is customary to thank a member of the funeral team with small monetary gifts.

An important part of the funeral is the farewell dinner which takes place in a cafe or at home. This meal is never paid for through funeral agencies but constitutes a separate service. Memorial dinners are held either at home or in a café and last from two to four hours. The menu must include pancakes, rice with honey (called *kutia*), jelly, and cabbage soup. These dishes have a symbolic meaning and are intended to celebrate eternal life. During the funeral dinner, the guests remember the deceased and tell stories connected with them. Time taken to attend funerals is taken as unpaid leave.

9.6 Cultural differences

Funeral agencies in Russia constitute a secular type of service. Nevertheless, they always sell goods for various confessions: for example, instead of a wooden cross to the grave, they can offer a metal plate with a crescent. However, if religious requests differ significantly from an agency's list of services, then they may refuse to render service. Therefore, as a rule, various religious rites are organized by religious communities.

I should also note that there are a considerable number of small nations and ethnic groupings in Russia. They live away from big cities and include indigenous peoples such as the Chukchi and Tuvans and Turkic ethnic groups such as the Yakuts. These groups tend to live in sparsely-populated rural settlements in the non-European, eastern regions of Russia. Their culture is rather traditional and they follow traditional funeral practices including open-air cremation, tree burial, and burial in the tundra. It is impossible to quantify the numbers involved. These practices are formally illegal but not policed.

Notes

1 'Russians are dying more often at home'. https://newizv.ru/news/society/01-11-2016/248572-rossijane-stali-chashe-umirat-doma acc. May 25, 2021.
2 'Russians die in hospitals'. www.rbc.ru/economics/13/04/2015/5527c12f9a79477a349f08f7 acc. May 25, 2021.
3 More than 60 percent of bodies are autopsied in Russia. Autopsies increase the opportunity to sell informal services inside the morgue (for example, preparing the body after an autopsy) which is an informal business for government mortuary workers.

10 Funeral costs

10.1 The value of the funeral industry

The value of the Russian funeral market is officially estimated at 65 billion ₽ ($0.9bn) a year, plus another 250 billion ₽ ($3.5bn) in the shadow economy in 2019–2020.[1] According to my estimates, the share of the shadow economy is about 300 billion ₽ ($4bn) if the figure includes the cost of production and installation of monuments, as well as corruption in morgues and hospitals.

The ten largest funeral companies in Russia officially earned 6.6 billion ₽ ($92m) in 2018; sales of the top 100 companies amounted to 14.46 billion ₽ ($195m) and the top 1000 amounted to 23.72 billion ₽ ($400m). Accordingly, about 210 billion ₽ are distributed among thousands of other players, including those in the shadow market. Significant single players are listed in Table 10.1.

Table 10.1 Significant operators in the Russian funeral market[2]

Company	Location	Revenue in 2020 (₽)	Ownership
'Ritual Service'	Moscow	1.2 bn	Public
'Honest Agent'	Moscow	776m	Private
St Petersburg Ritual Company	St Petersburg	447m	Public
Kirovo-Chepetsky Ritual Company	Kirovsk	431m	Public-private
R.I.P.	St Petersburg	408m	Public-private
Ritual.ru	Moscow	343m	Public-private

Sources: (1) Funeral market in Russia https://marketing.rbc.ru/research/40570/ acc. May 25, 2021; (2) Russian funeral market: current situation and main players https://marketing.rbc.ru/research/44227/ acc. May 25, 2021; (3) Funeral companies ranking by revenue www.testfirm.ru/rating/96_03/ acc. May 25, 2021.

DOI: 10.4324/9781003153672-10

An estimated 3,000 firms and 5,000 small entrepreneurs are engaged in the funeral industry, and about 40,000 people are not officially registered. Official statistics are much more modest and recognize about 1,000 established companies, 70 percent of which are private businesses, and about 30 percent state municipal services.

A small funeral agency conducts an average of 5–10 funerals per month. A large regional funeral agency conducts around 120–150 funerals per month. Regional differences are significant. In some regions, the funeral market is under the total control of local municipalities (for example, Rostov-on-Don or Kazan); in others, municipalities do not participate in funeral preparations, and the market is divided by dozens of players (Kaluga). For the most part, funeral services in big cities tend to be monopolized, and there is a high degree of competition in medium and small cities. It is also worth considering that in regions with predominantly Islamic populations (the Caucasus – Dagestan, Chechnya, Ingushetia) the funeral market does not exist at all, as there are no specialized services. In these places, the local religious communities take charge of funeral arrangements.

10.2 Average funeral costs

We do not have accurate data on the average cost of a funeral because informal payments are high. This applies to payments at the cemetery and morgue and includes the payment of police services from funeral agencies for information. However, researchers and experts still offer some estimates. According to them, the average cost of a funeral in the city is 70,000 ₽ ($950). In Moscow and St. Petersburg the cost is higher at around 120,000 ₽ ($1300), and in the countryside much lower at 30,000 ₽ ($ 400). This price does not include the purchase of a burial plot in the cemetery. The cost equals 2 times the average wage in the city and 1.5 average wages in the countryside.[3] The high cost of funerals and especially the large share of shadow payments are a constant source of criticism in the media.

It is crucial to mention that the state returns part of the funds spent on the funeral (funeral allowance). In each region, the amount returned varies. In Moscow it constitutes about 18,400₽ ($220), while in Russia outside the capital it is approximately 7,500₽ ($100). Around 10 percent of funerals in Russia are held solely at the expense of the state.

10.3 Funeral director fixed costs

The main source of income for a funeral director comes from the sale of fixed costs including

- Paperwork;
- Funeral transport services; and
- Mediation in informal services: between family members and employees of the morgue, cemetery.

Usually, such compulsory fees are 10,000–20,000 ₽ ($120–280).

10.4 Funeral director variable costs

It is difficult to measure the cost of each funeral. One can only average the amounts since in each case everything depends on the set of services chosen, burial place, and informal fees. I will provide the whole list, focusing on open data and personal research experience. The average range of costs, comparing burial and cremation, is given in Table 10.2. This does not include the cost of memorials: a basic wooden cross costs 10,000–15,000₽ ($50–150), and a basic stone monument costs 15,000–30,000 ₽ ($200–400). A more elaborate monument with a flower garden and a small sculpture costs between 15,000 and 130,000₽ ($500–1,500), and larger individual memorial sculptures can cost between 350,000 and 750,000 ₽ ($5,000–10,000).

The purchasing power of the Russian population is quite low. The figures given include informal fees, and in each case they may vary. In rural regions and small cities, most commonly, people do not pay for a place in a cemetery, and the coffin is bought cheaply.

10.5 Cemetery costs

As I have mentioned, providing a place in a cemetery is a public good. Receiving a free burial plot means that the municipality decides in which cemetery the plot is located and what kind of place it will be. The family has no opportunity to influence the selection. These plots are not a private property: rather, the family has leased the right to bury in a particular place.

On the shadow market, a place in a prestigious cemetery in Moscow can be obtained by bidding for the old burial. Relatives of the deceased may deal with the resale of old leases. For example, they are now offering to sell the right to bury in old graves at Vagankovsky, Danilovsky, and other Moscow cemeteries. A burial plot at the Vagankovsky Cemetery costs 1.7 million ₽s ($25,000 dollars), at Danilovsky and Ostankino 1.2 million ₽s ($15,000), and at Kalitnikovsky Cemetery 700,000 ₽s ($10,000).

One can also buy (to take over the lease) a place in a small provincial cemetery. A good place in a cemetery can cost 30,000 ₽s–100,000 ₽s ($500–1,200). Buying a 'good place' will guarantee that the plot will not

Table 10.2 Average costs: burial and cremation (₽ and $)

Burial		Cremation	
Transportation of the body from the place of death to the morgue	3,500–13,000 ₽ ($50–150)	Transportation of the body from the place of death to the morgue	3,500–13,000 ₽ ($50–150)
Coffin with all accessories	3,500–30,000 ₽ ($50–360)	Coffin with all accessories	3,500–30,000 ₽ ($50–350)
Wreath on the grave	500–1,500 ₽ ($8–20)		
Temporary cross	750–2,300 ₽ ($10–30)		
Hearse	7,500–20,000 ₽ ($10–280)	Hearse	7,500–20,000 ₽ ($10–280)
Funeral services (including paperwork)	10,000–20,000 ₽ ($120–280)	Funeral services (including paperwork)	10,000–20,000 ₽ ($120–280)
Body preparation in the morgue (with embalming)	12,000–35,000 ₽ ($150–500)	Body preparation in the morgue (without embalming)	7,500–20,000 ₽ ($150–300)
Priest	3,500–10,000 ₽ ($50–150)	Priest	3,500–10,000 ₽ ($50–150)
Official purchase of family plot (if you don't like a free burial plot and would like to buy a family plot)	220,000–1,500,000 ₽ ($3,000–15,000)	Crematorium services	15,000–30,000 ₽ ($200–400)
Cemetery place (informal fee)	12,000–35,000 ₽ ($150–500)		12,000–35,000 ₽ ($150–500)
Grave digging (summer)	5,000–14,000 ₽ ($80–130)		
Grave digging (winter)	7,500–25,000 ₽ ($100–300)	Urn burial in the grave	5,000–7,500 ₽ ($80–100)
Burial plot preparation	5,000–7,500 ₽ ($80–100)	Purchase of niche in columbarium	5,000–15,000 ₽ ($80–200)
Funeral dinner for ten people (without the hire and decoration)	12,000–35,000 ₽ ($150–500)	Funeral dinner for ten people (without the hire and decoration)	12,000–35,000 ₽ ($150–500)
Total average[4]	70,000–200,000 ₽ ($900–2,500)	**Total average**	35,000–65,000 ₽ ($500–900)

get flooded with water or that a tree will not fall on it. These resale practices are illegal, and common in the shadow funeral market. In Russia, there is no practice of exhumation in the event of burial taking place illegally, and no formal punishment.

10.6 Municipal funeral services

The state provides citizens with a minimum set of funeral services free of charge. Relatives can choose these services and receive them, or they can choose to receive a cash payment. This payment is about 15,000 ₽s for Moscow and about 7–8 ₽s for the regions. Also, there is an option to purchase services additional to the minimum set, for example, a coffin or transportation vehicle. The difference in cost is paid by the buyer.

10.7 Funeral planning and insurance

Most Russians do not specially prepare for death. Funeral pre-planning is very poorly developed. Funeral planning and insurance are provided by a number of insurance companies and large funeral players (for example, *Ritual. ru*). Since 2017, the possibility of introducing compulsory funeral insurance for all citizens of the Russian Federation has been actively discussed as a measure to remove corruption from the funeral market. As of 2021 this proposal has not been put into mass practice.

According to mass polls[5] about 25 percent of people over 65 save money for funerals. Most have them saved around $1,000-$1,500 and store this money in banks or at home in cash.

Notes

1 Paid Services to the Population. State Statistics Service. https://rosstat.gov.ru/storage/mediabank/Plat_obsluj-2019.pdf acc. May 25, 2021.
2 Figures may differ from reality. Many funeral companies use several legal entities at once, while being one company.
3 Federal State Statistics Service. Socio-economic Situation in Russia. https://rosstat.gov.ru/storage/mediabank/fU7e3uMD/osn-01-2021.pdf acc. May 25, 2021.
4 Excluding the purchase of a place for a family burial plot.
5 'Passive aging and active longevity: Practices and politics'. https://social.ranepa.ru/novosti/item/issledovanie-ekspertov-ranhigs-passivnoe-starenie-i-aktivnoe-dolgoletie acc. May 25, 2021.

11 Commemoration and remembrance in the public sphere

11.1 Gravestones

Immediately after the funeral, a temporary memorial sign is placed on the grave. It takes about a year before the installation of the tombstone. Most commonly, a temporary sign is a wooden cross with a sign where the name is indicated but can also be just an iron plate. The cost of a temporary sign on the grave is approximately 3,700 ₽ ($50).

A year later, a monument is selected and put up. The erection of the monument is an integral part of the funeral cycle. The selection and installation of the monument are taken seriously. The monument can be made of concrete, granite, marble, or basalt, but the most common material is Karelian granite.

The cost of the monument starts at $150 for a small granite monument. Engraving, pedestal, and installation of the monument are added to this value. The total cost is about $250. The average cost of a monument in Russia is about $800-$1,200.

The geographical location of the workshop and cemetery greatly influences the price of the monument. The monuments are cheaper the closer the workshop is to the quarry. Therefore, for example, in the southern regions of Russia (close to the Crimea) and the northern (close to Karelia) the monuments in the cemetery will be larger in size than in central Russia.

Tombstones of members of criminal gangs are a vital part of the culture of death in post-Soviet Russia. As a phenomenon, these gravestones appeared at the very end of the 1980s, when Perestroika was started in the USSR. Early purchasers included newly rich businessmen and members of criminal gangs. Gang members who had been killed were often honored with large tombstones that were very different from Soviet self-made ones: the monuments were made of stone and were large in size. They often depicted various attributes of criminal life – expensive cars, jewelry. In many ways,

DOI: 10.4324/9781003153672-11

the growing popularity of installation of such tombstones is associated with the emergence of the market after the collapse of the USSR.

11.2 Memory days

The *pominki* (wake) is a special ritual of memory of the dead. Pominki includes several actions. First, people go to church. Typically, this is a church next to the cemetery. Relatives light candles in memory of the dead and order a memorial service. It takes no more than half an hour. Second, people gathering at the cemetery. Guests eat and drink at the grave of a relative and clean up at the grave. Common foods for commemoration are sweets, sandwiches, eggs, vodka and beer, and compotes. Guests also bring millet or grains for feeding the birds. Guests leave part of the food at the grave. This second part lasts one to two hours. On such days, hundreds of people can gather at the cemetery at the same time.

Pominki takes place on specific days of the year. The principal days are at Radonitsa, which takes place on the second weekend after Easter. The more common name for these memory days is 'parental Saturdays', which means that people have to remember their dead kin on these days. In the Russian Orthodox Church, the special memory days also include Saturdays on the second, third, and fourth week of Great Lent.

These holidays are significant in the Russian culture of death. The owner-less condition of many cemeteries has led to the practice of visiting the cemetery on these days for cleaning and repairing graves. People paint fences, clear away dead leaves, and plant flowers. These repair practices are the memorial ritual inherited from the Soviet and post-Soviet culture of death. Researchers argue that repairing and maintaining the infrastructure of the cemetery these days has ritual significance. Thus, every year, relatives find exactly what needs to be repaired at the cemetery.

Memorial days are never held at home but families generally have photographs of the dead people at home. Communication with the dead occurs only in the cemetery and during church services. Traditionally, during any formal dinner, the second toast is devoted to the dead.

In 2014, the Public Opinion Foundation conducted a nationwide survey on visits to cemeteries.[1] The vast majority of citizens (67 percent) visit cemeteries three to five times a year. In villages and small towns, people attend cemetery more often than in big cities (6–8 times versus 2–4 times). At the same time, 30 percent go specifically to maintain graves in cemeteries and 45 percent to express their memory and respect for deceased relatives. Older people are more likely to be frequent visitors; young people under the age of 35 believe that the cemetery is not a very pleasurable place and they tend to visit it less often.

Figure 11.1 The annual painting of fences and tombstones for Easter is an important element of communication with the dead. In the picture, the daughter and mother of the author of the book paint the fences at the family burial plot.

Source: Moscow, Rogozhskoe cemetery. 2017.

11.3 Spontaneous shrines

There is a common practice of installing spontaneous roadside memorials at the place of death – often as a result of car accidents. These memorials have no legal standing and are generally limited to wreaths, mourning ribbons, flowers, and sometimes photographs. Visually, some of the shrines often look like ordinary Russian burial plots with gravestones, fences, and a grave mound and may include car parts: most often, it is the steering wheel, which becomes a part of such a shrine. Some funeral agencies offer the service of building roadside memorials.

Most shrines are maintained over long periods. The long-term existence of such shrines is made possible by the fact that many roads are ownerless. Spontaneous shrines on the roadside can be found in many countries of Eastern Europe, including Ukraine, Belarus, Romania, Greece, Poland, and Lithuania.

11.4 Unknown burial places, reburials, and war memorial days

In early 2019, the Ministry of Defense reported that last year the number of certified burial sites of the Great Patriotic War reached 32,000. According to military commissions, about one and a half million soldiers of the Red Army remain unburied.[2] On July 23, 2019, the government approved the federal target program 'Perpetuating the memory of those who died while defending the Fatherland for 2019–2024'. The program has three main objectives: searching for unknown graves, reburial and arrangement of new burial plots, and repair and maintenance of military graves. The post-Soviet culture of death entails the practice of searching unknown soldiers' graves.[3]

Search and reburials are operated mainly by activists and volunteers, using archives, maps, and testimonies. Activists are not only engaged in reburials but also create local memorial museums, participate in the installation of monuments and publish memorial books. There are around 60,000 such volunteers. The culture of search and reburial is developed in former battle places in Central Russia, Belarusia, and the Ukraine. Many funeral agencies are involved in reburials, charging minimal or no fee. World War II plays a structural role in the culture of death in post-Soviet Russia. Each village will generally have monuments to soldiers and their mothers. Days of Remembrance are held each year and incorporate the laying of flowers around the monuments.

At the same time, attempts being made to locate and rebury the victims of political repressions, mainly of the Stalin period of the 1930–1950s, have faced serious state resistance. Activists are often denied access to the archives and prohibited from the installation of commemorative signs. The historian Yuri Dmitriev, who found the place of execution of political prisoners in Sandarmokh, is under criminal prosecution.[4]

Another essential element of post-Soviet death culture is the reburial of the remains of politicians, actors, and writers. In the 1990s, the remains of the imperial Romanov family were found and reburied.[5] Over the past 15 years, the repatriation has taken place of the remains of the emigrants of the Civil War including General A. Denikin and the philosopher I. Ilyin, who was exhumed in Switzerland and reburied with high honors at the prestigious Don Necropolis.[6]

Figure 11.2 & Figure 11.3 Reburial of the remains of unknown soldiers. Reburial of the remains of unknown soldiers. The color of the fabric inside the coffin is usually red or purple. These are the colors of the Soviet army.

Source: Photo from the author's own collection.

11.5 Public mourning: terrorism and mass disasters

Post-Soviet Russia has been subject to many terrorist attacks: several thousands have taken place over the last 30 years. Of these, the deadliest events included:

- A series of explosions of residential buildings in Buinaksk, Volgodonsk, Moscow (1999) – 303 dead;
- Hostage-taking in the theater on Dubrovka (2002) – 174 dead;
- The explosion at the rock festival 'Wings' (2003) – 15 dead;
- The capture of the school in Beslan (2004) – 333 dead, mostly children;
- Explosions in the Moscow metro (2010) – 44 dead;
- Explosion at Domodedovo Airport (2011) – 38 dead; and
- Explosion in the metro of St. Petersburg (2017) – 16 dead.

The attacks had a great influence on post-Soviet society. However, no annual mourning days are devoted to the people who died in these attacks. Only relatives of the deceased bring flowers to the places of memory. Large memorial signs or official monuments have been installed at some sites of terrorist attacks. Such signs were installed at the site of the terrorist bombings of houses on the Kashirskoye highway and near the theater center on Dubrovka.

Notes

1 Sociological Service Report. Practices and Meanings of Visiting Cemeteries. https://fom.ru/TSennosti/11810 acc. April 6, 2021. Telephone survey of citizens of the Russian Federation 18 years of age and older on a random sample of mobile and landline phone numbers. 320 cities, 160 villages, 1000 respondents. The statistical error does not exceed 3.8 percent. The poll was posted on April 13, 2014.
2 'Army of the unknown. How many soldiers who gave their lives for their Motherland during the Great Patriotic War have not yet been recognized?'. www.kommersant.ru/doc/4088260 acc.April 6, 2021.
3 J. Dahlin (2018) '"Now you have visited the war": The search for fallen soldiers in Russia', in M. Frihammar and H. Silverman (eds.) *Heritage of Death: Landscapes of Emotion, Memory and Practice*. London: Routledge, 131–144.
4 'Yuri Dmitriev: Chronicle of the criminal prosecution'. https://zona.media/theme/dmitriev acc. April 6, 2021.
5 There are still disputes about the exact belonging of the remains to the Romanov family. The royal family was shot during the October Revolution and the exact burial place was unknown.
6 All of these practices are well described in N. Tumarkin (1994) *The Living and the Dead: The Rise and Fall of the Cult of World War II in Russia*. New York, NY: Basic Books and K. Verdery (1999) *The Political Lives of Dead Bodies: Reburial and Postsocialist Change*. New York: Columbia University Press.

References

'Army of the unknown: How many soldiers who gave their lives for their Mother-land during the Great Patriotic War have not yet been recognized?'. www.kommersant.ru/doc/4088260 acc. 6 April 2021.

Barthel, G. (1925) 'K postroike v Moskve pervogo v SSSR krematoriya' [Construction in Moscow of the first Soviet crematorium], *Kommunal'noe khozyaistvo* [Communal economy], 23, 25–37.

Becker, C., Mendelsohn, J. and Benderskaya, K. (2012) *Russian Urbanization in the Soviet and Post-Soviet Eras*. London. http://pubs.iied.org/pdfs/10613IIED.pdf acc. 18 May 2020.

Binns, C. (1979) 'The changing face of power: Revolution and accommodation in the development of the Soviet ceremonial system. Part I', *Man* (New series), 14, 585–606.

Binns, C. (1980) 'The changing face of power: Revolution and accommodation in the development of the Soviet ceremonial system. Part II', *Man* (New series), 15, 170–187.

Boylan, S. (1996) 'Organized crime and corruption in Russia: Implications for U.S. and international law', *Fordham International Law Journal*, 19:5, 1999–2027.

Bremer, T. (2013) *Cross and Kremlin: A Brief History of the Orthodox Church in Russia*. Grand Rapids, MI: Eerdmans.

Causes of Mortality in Russia. Demoscope. www.demoscope.ru/weekly/2020/0849/barom04.php acc. 18 May 2021.

'A coffin, a cemetery, hundreds of billions of rubles: How bureaucrats, siloviki and thugs divide the funeral market'. https://novayagazeta.ru/articles/2019/06/08/80819-grob-kladbische-sotni-milliardov-rubley acc. 6 April 2021.

Collins, S. (1671/2008) *The Present State of Russia*. Edited by M. Poe. London: Iowa Research Online.

'Complete sets and photos can be found on the website of one of the manufacturers'. https://luidorbus.ru/product/ritualnyy-transport/ritualnyy-avtobus-gazel-next/ acc. 6 April 2021.

Comprehensive Monitoring of the Living Conditions of the Population. www.gks.ru/free_doc/new_site/KOUZ18/index.html acc. 18 May 2021.

'Cremation is cheaper than burial'. www.kommersant.ru/doc/1952216 acc. 6 April 2021.

Dahlin, J. (2018) '"Now you have visited the war": The search for fallen soldiers in Russia', in M. Frihammar and H. Silverman (eds.) *Heritage of Death: Landscapes of Emotion, Memory and Practice*. London: Routledge, 131–144.

Doklad komissii o narodnom zdravii po zakonoproektu ob ustroistve kladbishch i krematoriev, o pogrebenii i registratsii umershikh [The report of the Commission on the people's health on the draft law on the structure of cemeteries and crematoria, burial, and registration of deaths]; Prilozheniya k stenograficheskim otchetam Gosudarstvennoi dumy. Vol. 6 (No. 556–643). Chetvertyi sozyv, 1913–1914 gg. Sessiya vtoraya [Annexes to the verbatim records of the State Duma. Vol. 6 (No. 556–643). The fourth convocation, 1913–1914 Session two]. SPb.: Gosudarstvennaya typografia, No. 579.

The Economist Intelligence Unit. Global Health Care. https://eiuperspectives.econ omist.com/sites/default/files/Globalaccesstohealthcare-3.pdf acc. 18 May 2021.

The Economist Intelligence Unit. The Quality of Life Index 2013. www.economist. com/news/2012/11/21/the-lottery-of-life acc. 18 May 2021.

Employment and Unemployment in the Russian Federation in February 2020. https://gks.ru/bgd/free/B04_03/IssWWW.exe/Stg/d05/53.htm acc. 18 May 2020.

Federal Service for State Registration. Cadastre and Cartography. https://ros reestr.ru/site/activity/gosudarstvennoe-upravlenie-v-sfere-ispolzovaniya-i-okhrany-zemel/gosudarstvennyy-monitoring-zemel/sostoyanie-zemel-rossii/gosudarstvennyy-natsionalnyy-doklad-o-sostoyanii-i-ispolzovanii-zemel-v-ros siyskoy-federatsii/ acc. 18 May 2020.

Federal State Statistics Service. www.gks.ru/folder/313/document/72529 acc. 18 May 2021.

Federal State Statistics Service. Socio-Economic Situation in Russia. https://rosstat. gov.ru/storage/mediabank/fU7e3uMD/osn-01-2021.pdf acc. 25 May 2021.

The funeral financial support by state is carried out at the expense of the respective budgets following Articles 9, 10, 11 of this Federal Law.

Freeze, Gregory L. (2008) 'Recent scholarship on Russian Orthodoxy: A critique', *Kritika: Explorations in Russian and Eurasian History*, 2:2, 269–278.

Gizieva, K. (2016) 'Gorodskoj pogrebal'nyj obrjad vtoroj poloviny xix – nachala HH veka (na primere Omska)', *Manuskript*, 12:2, 74.

Gregory, P. (1976) '1913 Russian national income: Some insights into Russian economic development', *The Quarterly Journal of Economics*, 90:3, 445–459.

Grossman, G. (1960) *Soviet Statistics of Physical Output of Industrial Commodities: Their Compilation and Quality*. Princeton, NJ: Princeton University Press.

Hosking, G. (1997) *Russia: People and Empire, 1552–1917*. Cambridge: Harvard University Press.

'In the Kirov region, pagans burned the body of a colleague on a funeral pyre'. www. mk.ru/social/2018/03/05/v-kirovskoy-oblasti-yazychniki-sozhgli-telo-soratnika-na-pogrebalnom-kostre.html.

'"I will bury quickly and expensively": Who is fighting with the Russian Orthodox Church for the funeral market?'. https://ria.ru/20170830/1501342182.html acc. 28 April 2021.

Iz stenogrammy soveshchaniia po problemam memorial'noi arkhitektury [From the transcript of the colloquium on the questions of memorial architecture]. 3–5 iiunia 1946 g. In Sovetskoe izobrazitel'noe iskusstvo i arkhitektura 60-kh – 70-kh godov [Soviet representational art and architecture of the 1960–1970-s, A collection of articles]. Moscow, Nauka Publishers, 1979. Zadachi arkhitektorov v dni Velikoi Otechestvennoi voiny. Materialy 10 plenuma pravleniia SSA SSSR 22–25 aprelia 1942 g. [Tasks of the architects in the days of the Great Patriotic War, Acts of 10th plenary session of the administration of the Union of Soviet Architects of the USSR]. Moscow, Gos. arhitekturnoe izd-vo Akademii arhitektury SSSR, 1942.

Kaiser, D. (1992) 'Death and dying in early modern Russia', in N. S. Kollman (ed.) *Major Problems in Early Modern Russian History*. London: Garland, 217–258.

Kotkin, S. (1997) *Magnetic Mountain: Stalinism as a Civilization*. Oakland, CA: University of California Press.

Krivosheev, G. (1997) *Soviet Casualties and Combat Losses in the Twentieth Century*. Barnsley: Greenhill Books, 85.

Kudukin, P. (2012) '"Proizvodstvennaja kvaziobshhina kak centr zhiznennogo mira", cited in The USSR: Life after Death (collection of articles ed. by I.V. Glushchenko, B.Y. Kagarlitsky, V.A. Kurennoj)', *Topos*, 1, 152–157.

Ledeneva, A. (2008) '"Blat" and "guanxi": Informal practices in Russia and China', *Comparative Studies in Society and History*, 50:1, 118–144.

List of people cryopreserved in 'KrioRus'. http://kriorus.ru/Krionirovannye-lyudi acc. 6 April 2021.

Logunova, M. (2010) 'Traurnyj ceremonial v Rossijskoj imperii', *Vlast*, 3, 3–13.

Logunova, M. (2017). 'Pechal'nye ritualy imperatorskoj Rossii', *Centrpoligraf*, 317.

Lovell, S., Rogachevskii, A. and Ledeneva, A. (eds.) (2000) *Bribery and Blat in Russia: Negotiating Reciprocity from the Early Modern Period to the 1990s*. London: Palgrave Macmillan, 312.

Malinina, T. (2018) 'Cultural palimpsests: Their manifestation and reading in the architectural and artistic texts of the Soviet era', *Artikult*, 29:1, 75–96.

McDowell, J. (1974) 'Soviet civil ceremonies', *Journal for the Scientific Study of Religion*, 13:3, 265–279.

Merridale, C. (2002) *Night of Stone: Death and Memory in Twentieth-Century Russia*. Harmsworth: Penguin Books.

'Ministry of Construction proposes to seize and cremate remains from abandoned graves' [Минстрой предлагает изымать и кремировать останки из заброшенных могил]. https://iz.ru/news/584670.

Mironov, B. (2012) 'Gorod iz derevni: chetyresta let rossijskoj urbanizacii', *Otechestvennye zapiski*, 3:48, 111.

Mokhov, S. (2021) *Archeology of Russian Death: Ethnography of the Funeral Industry in Contemporary Russia*. Moscow: Common Place (Мохов С. Археология русской смерти. Этнография похоронного дела в современной России. Москва: Common place, 2021).

Mokhov, S. and Sokolova, A. (2020) 'Broken infrastructure and soviet modernity: The funeral market in Russia', *Mortality*, 25:2, 232–248.

Mokhov, S. and Zotova, V. (2017) 'The case of the fence, table and bench: Modes of justice in the practice of allocating places in a cemetery', *Journal of Social Policy Research*, 15:1, 21–36. (Мохов С. В., Зотова В. Дело об ограде, столике и скамье: режимы справедливости в практиках распределения мест на кладбище // Журнал исследований социальной политики. 2017. Т. 15. No 1. С. 21–36).

Molyarenko, O. (2017a) 'Ownerless highways in Russia', *ECO*, 4:514, 88–109. (Моляренко О. А. Бесхозяйные автомобильные дороги в России // ЭКО. 2017. № 4 (514). С. 88–109).

Molyarenko, O. (2017b) 'State practices of constructing statistical illusions, or "dead zones" of domestic statistics', *Sociological Journal*, 23:4, 104–120. (Моляренко О. А. Государственные практики конструирования статистических иллюзий, или "мёртвые зоны" отечественной статистики // Социологический журнал. 2017. Т. 23. № 4. С. 104–120).

Nefedova, T. (2001) 'Blagoustroistvo gorodov i selskoi mestnosti. Derevnia v gorode', in T. Nefedova, G. P. M. Polyan and A. I. Treivish (eds.) *Gorod i derevnya v Evropeiskoi Rossii: Sto let peremen*. Moscow: OGI, 400–413.

'The number of atheists in Russia has doubled in four years'. www.rbc.ru/society/2 3/03/2021/6059a2fd9a7947c314aab9c4 acc. 28 April 2021.

'The opinion of the inhabitants of Moscow about the funeral industry in the city'. www.mos.ru/upload/documents/files/1676/ritual.pdf acc. 6 April 2021.

Orlov, I. (2015) *Kommunal'naia strana. Stanovlenie sovetskogo zhilishchnokommu nal'nogo khoziaistva (1917–1941)*. Moscow: HSE University Press.

Paid services to the population. State Statistics Service. https://rosstat.gov.ru/storage/ mediabank/Plat_obsluj-2019.pdf acc. 25 May 2021.

'Passive aging and active longevity: Practices and politics'. https://social.ranepa. ru/novosti/item/issledovanie-ekspertov-ranhigs-passivnoe-starenie-i-aktivnoe-dolgoletie acc. 25 May 2021.

Pavlenko, N. (2005) *Elizaveta Petrovna: V krugu muz i favoritov*. Moscow: AST, 122.

Pravdzik B. Krematsiya [Cremation]. SPb.: Tipo-litografiya, fototipiya of V. I. Schtain, 1892. 45.

Public television of Russia (2016) 'In the Rostov region, the farmer will sue the funeral home, which established a cemetery in his field' [В Ростовской области фермер будет судиться с похоронной конторой, которая устроила кладбище на его поле'. https://otr-online.ru/news/v-rostovskoi-oblasti-ppart-72360.html acc. 6 April 2021.

Putin's Russia: How It Rose, How It Is Maintained, and How It Might End. Edited by Leon Aron. Washington, DC: American Enterprise Institute, 2015.

Religious Belief and National Belonging in Central and Eastern Europe. www.pew forum.org/2017/05/10/religious-belief-and-national-belonging-in-central-and-eastern-europe/ acc. 18 May 2020.

Russian Provincial Necropolis/Comp. Compiled by Vladimir Sheremetyevsky, Reprint edition of 1914. St. Petersburg: Alfaret, 2006, 724, 1028.

'Russians are dying more often at home'. https://newizv.ru/news/society/01-11-2016/ 248572-rossijane-stali-chashe-umirat-doma acc. 25 May 2021.

'Russians die in hospitals'. www.rbc.ru/economics/13/04/2015/5527c12f9a79477a 349f08f7 acc. 25 May 2021.

Sanitary rules and norms 2.1.2882–11 'Hygienic requirements for the placement, operation and maintenance of cemeteries, buildings and infrastructure for funerals'. https://funeralportal.ru/ acc. 25 May 2021.

Scott, J. C. (1977) *The Moral Economy of the Peasant: Rebellion and Subsistence in Southeast Asia*. New Haven, CT: Yale University Press.

Siegelbaum, L. (2009) 'On the side: Car culture in the USSR, 1960s–1980s', *Technology and Culture*, 50:1, 1–23.

Sociological Service Report. Practices and Meanings of Visiting Cemeteries. https://fom.ru/TSennosti/11810 acc. 6 April 2021. Telephone survey of citizens of the Russian Federation 18 years of age and older on a random sample of mobile and landline phone numbers. 320 cities, 160 villages. 1000 respondents. The statistical error does not exceed 3.8%. The poll was posted on April 13, 2014.

Sokolova, A. (2013) '"Nel'zia, nel'zia novykh liudei khoronit' po-staromu!" Evoliutsiia pokhoronnogo obriada v Sovetskoi Rossii' ["It is impossible, it is impossible to bury new people in the old way!" Evolution of the funeral rite in Soviet Russia], *Otechest vennye zapiski*, 5:56, 191–208.

Sokolova, A. (2018) 'Novii mir i staraja smert: sudba kladbisch v sovetskikh gorogakh 1920–1930h godov' [New world and the old death: The fate of cemeteries in the Soviet cities of the 1920s–1930s], *Neprikosnovennyi zapas*, 117:1, 74–94.

Sokolova, A. (2019) 'Soviet funeral services: From moral economy to social welfare and back', *Revolutionary Russia*, 32:2, 251–271.

Syutkin, G. (2016) *Funeral Business Fundamentals*. Tutorial, Moscow: Infra-M, Alpha-M, 320. (Сюткин Г.Н. Основы ритуально-похоронного дела. Учебное пособие. – Москва:Инфра-М, Альфа-М, 2016.- 320с).

'These Russian companies are offering exotic funerals to send you off in style'. www.rbth.com/business/329484-exotic-funerals acc. 6 April 2021.

This happened at the same time with the European transfer of cemeteries outside the city – for example, in Paris, Vienna, Milan and so on. Mytum, H. (2003) 'The social history of the European cemetery', in C. D. Bryant (ed.) *Handbook of Death and Dying*, Vol. 2. Thousand Oaks: Sage, 801–810.

'This is a professional association of workers in the funeral industry, which was quite influential in the 2000s'. http://pohoronotrasl-souz.ru/ acc. 6 April 2021.

This statement is based on the author's own observations during field research, as well as on publications in the media. For example. https://cutt.ly/YdS7P67 acc. 25 May 2021.

Tumarkin, N. (1994) *The Living and the Dead: The Rise and Fall of the Cult of World War II in Russia*. New York, NY: Basic Books.

Verdery, K. (1999) *The Political Lives of Dead Bodies: Reburial and Postsocialist Change*. New York: Columbia University Press.

Wegren, S. K. (2005) *The Moral Economy Reconsidered: Russia's Search for Agrarian Capitalism*. New York: Palgrave Macmillan.

The World Factbook. Central Intelligence Agency. www.cia.gov/library/publica
tions/the-world-factbook/geos/rs.html acc. 18 May 2020.

XX Congress of the CPSU. Verbatim report. Moscow, 1956.

'Yuri Dmitriev: Chronicle of the criminal prosecution'. https://zona.media/theme/
dmitriev acc. 6 April 2021.

Zhivotov, N. (1895) *Among the Torches Men: Six Days in the Role of a Torch Bearer*.
Izd. Den: Saint-Petersburg.

Index

Note: Page numbers in *italics* indicate a figure and page numbers in **bold** indicate a table on the corresponding page.

Printed in the United States
by Baker & Taylor Publisher Services